GREATER BELFAST
STREET ATLAS

Contents

Layout of Map Pages	See Opposing Page
Greater Belfast Map Pages	2-44
City Centre Maps	Inside Back Cover + 18
Street Index	45-64
Road Map of Ireland	Back Cover

Legend

Motorway		Parks & Playing Fields	
Main Roads/Streets	MALONE ROAD	Water	
Other Roads/Streets	WILLOW STREET / WILLOW DRIVE	Railway Line & Station	
One Way Streets	← HOWARD ST	Built-up Areas	
Pedestrianised Streets	FOUNTAIN STREET	Public Buildings / Church	

Scale of maps is 1:15,000 (4.2 inches to 1 mile or 6.66cm to 1 kilometre)

0   250m   500m   750m   1km

© Causeway Press (N.I.) 2006

The maps on pages 2 to 44 are based upon the Ordnance Survey of Northern Ireland with the permission of the Controller of Her Majesty's Stationery Office. Crown Copyright reserved. Permit Number 60122

All rights reserved. No part of this publication may be reproduced, stored in a retrieval system, or transmitted in any form or by any means electronic, mechanical, photocopying, recording or otherwise, without prior permission of Causeway Press (N.I.).

Great care has been taken throughout this publication to be accurate but the publishers cannot accept responsibility for any errors which appear, or their consequences.

Printed by The Universities Press (Belfast) Ltd. Compiled by Paul Slevin. Comments, suggestions and inquiries should be sent to him at the address below.

Published by Causeway Press (N.I.), 17 Osborne Park, Bangor, N.Ireland BT20 3DJ. Phone UK 07768 172442.
E-mail paulslevin@talk21.com

Distributed by Eason Wholesale Books Ltd (phone Dublin 862 2111), and Argosy Libraries Ltd (phone Dublin 823 9500).
Quote ISBN 1 872600 24 7.

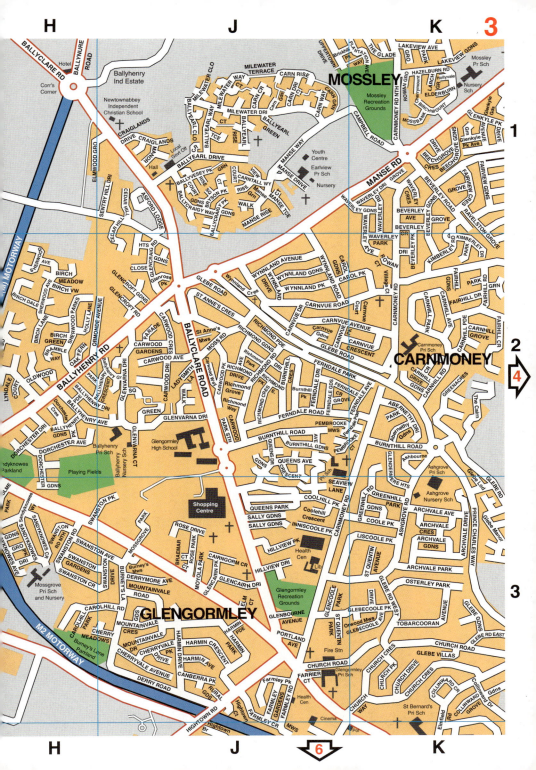

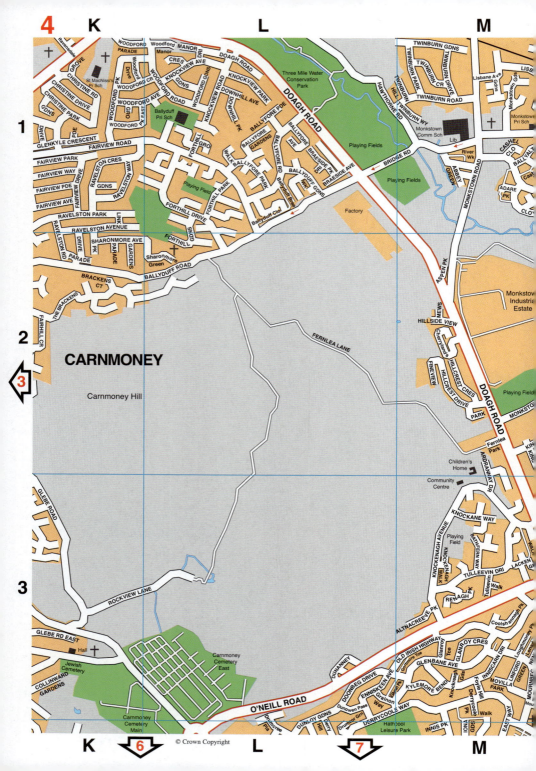

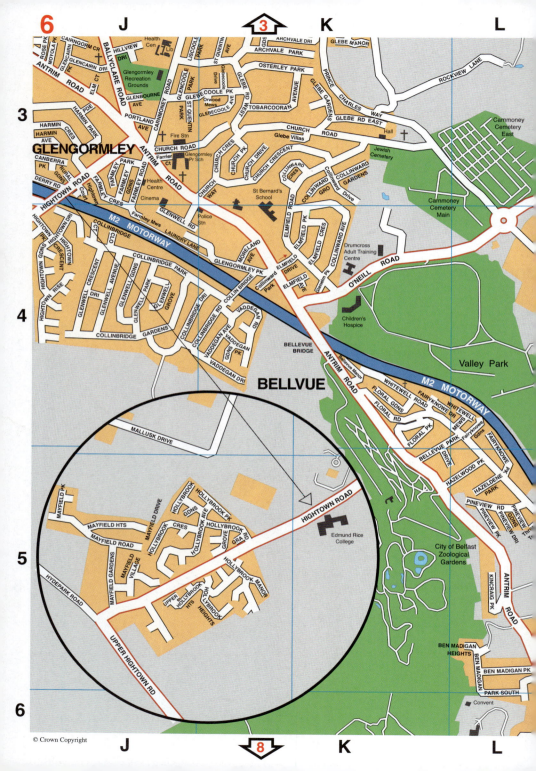

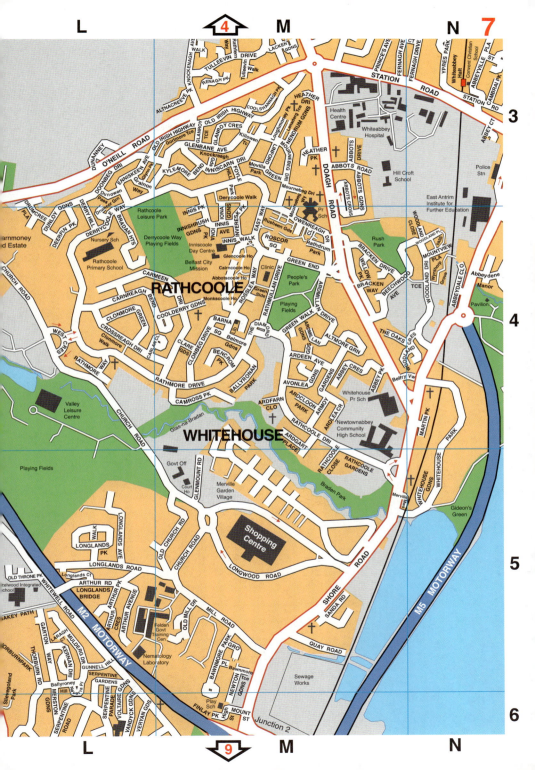

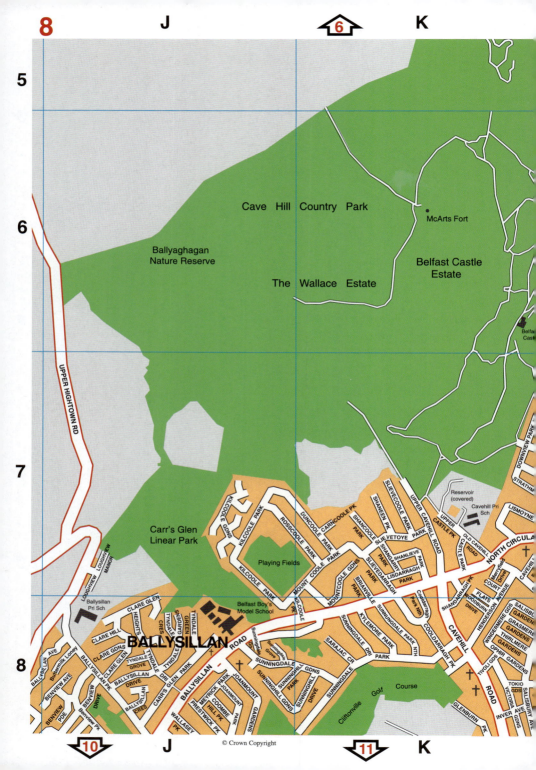

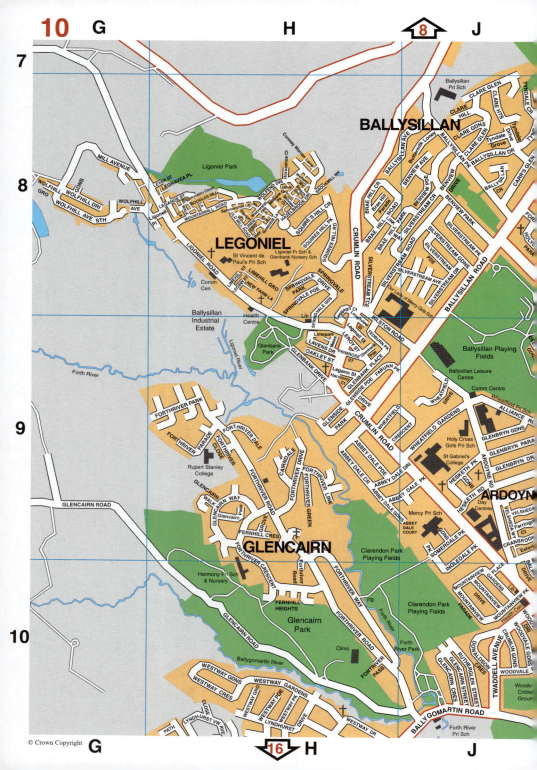

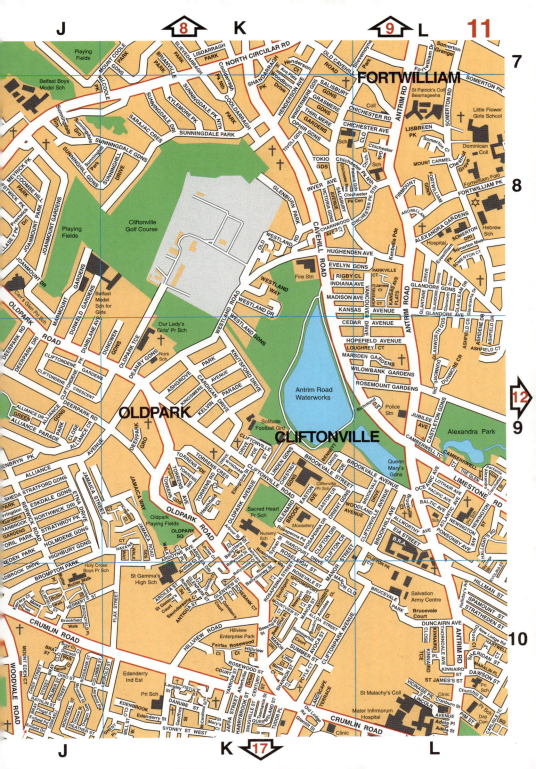

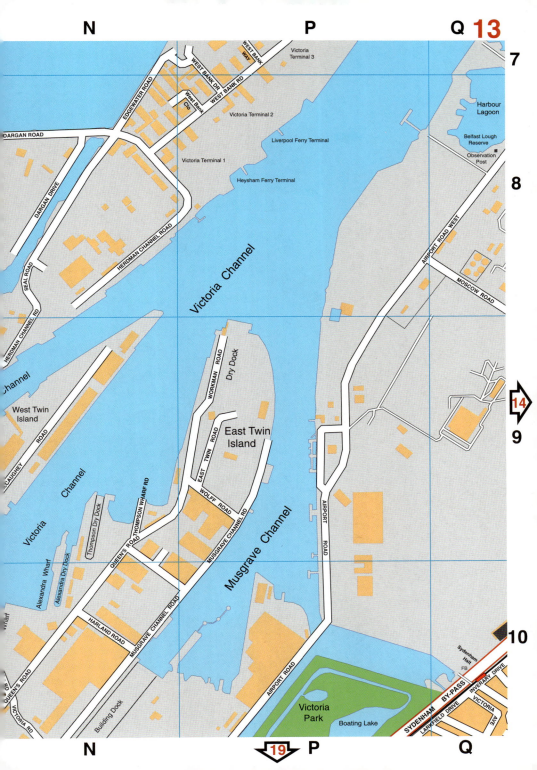

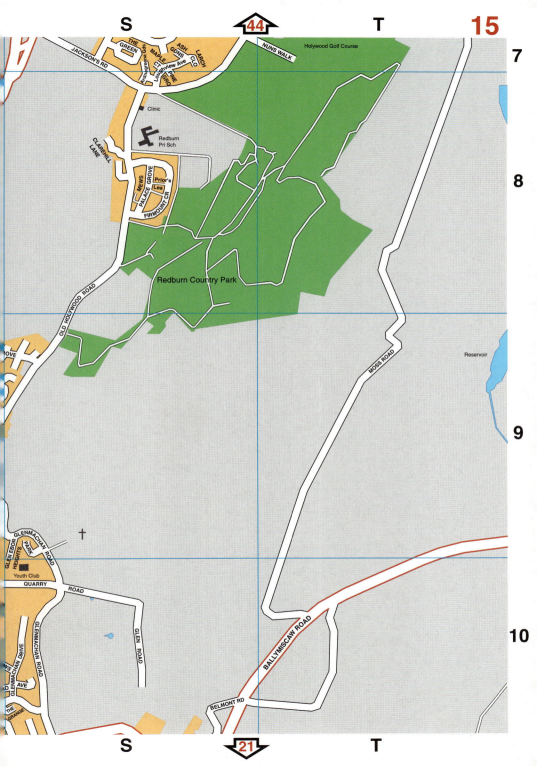

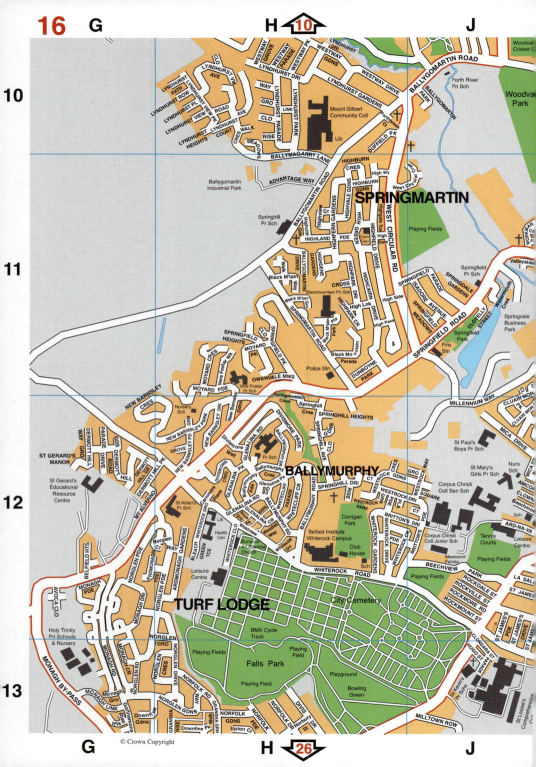

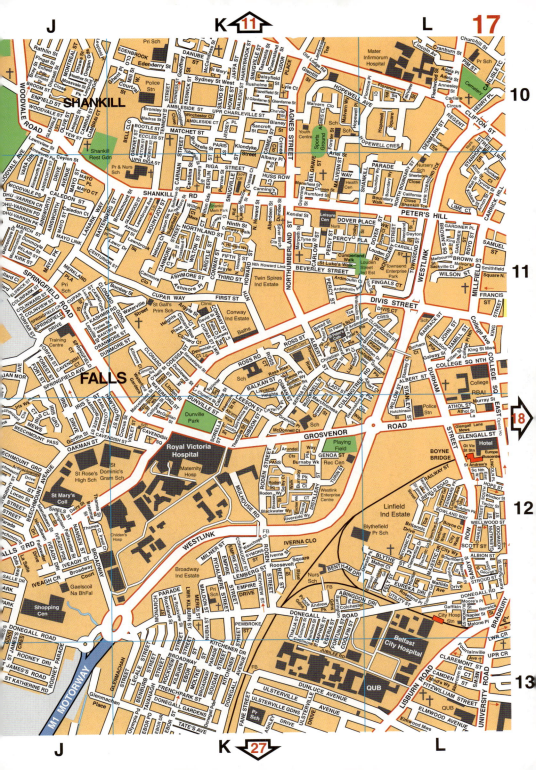

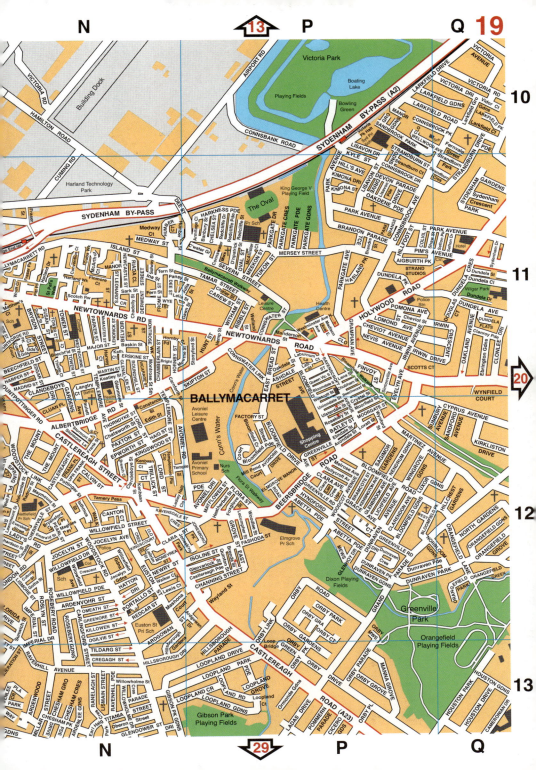

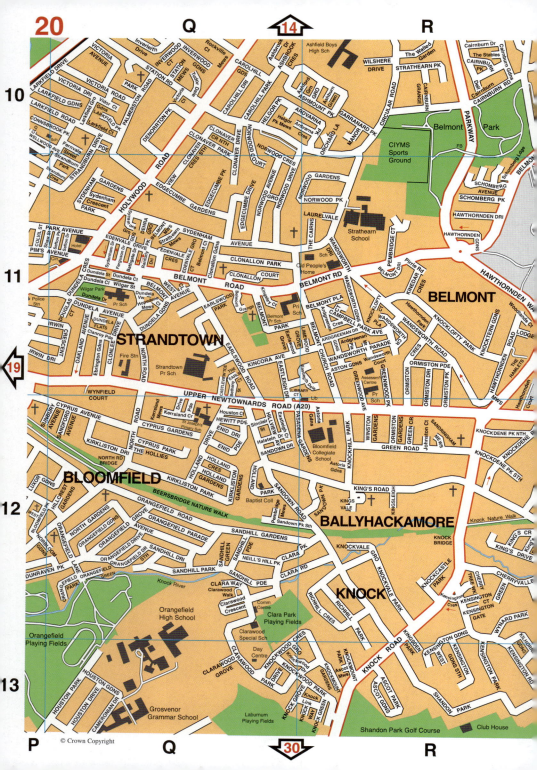

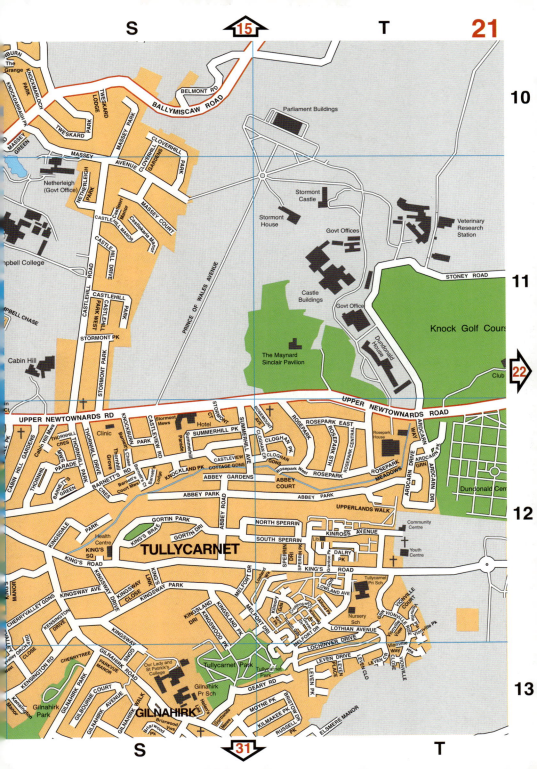

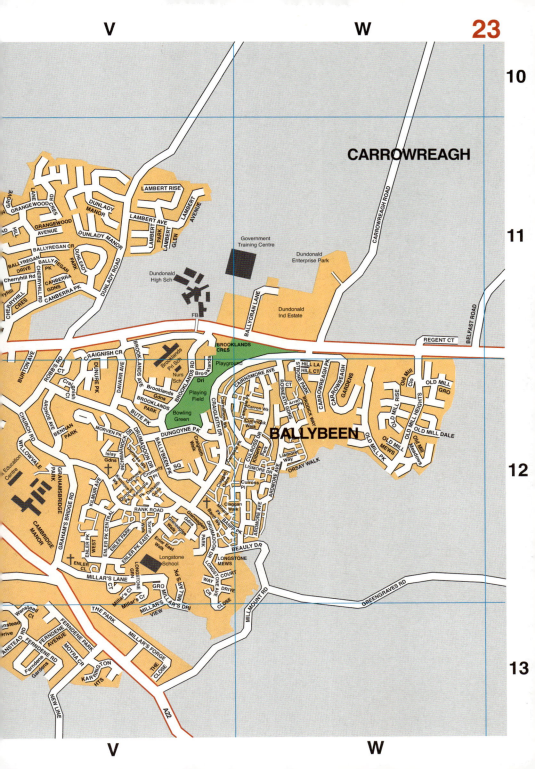

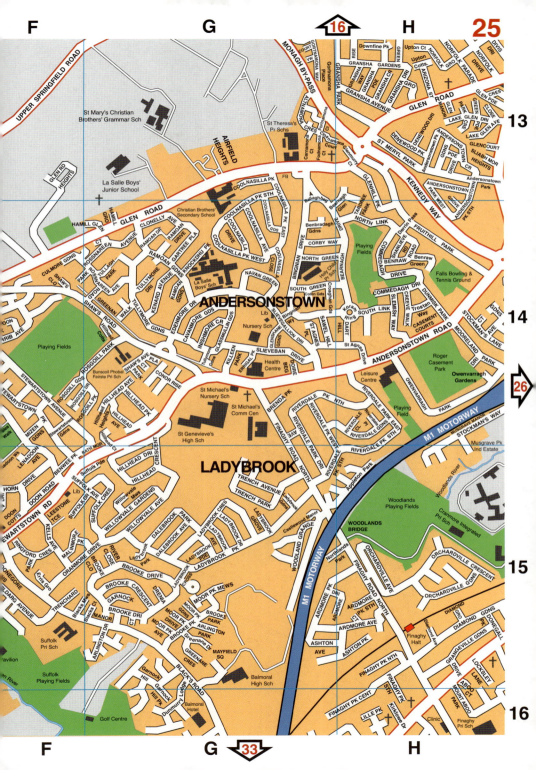

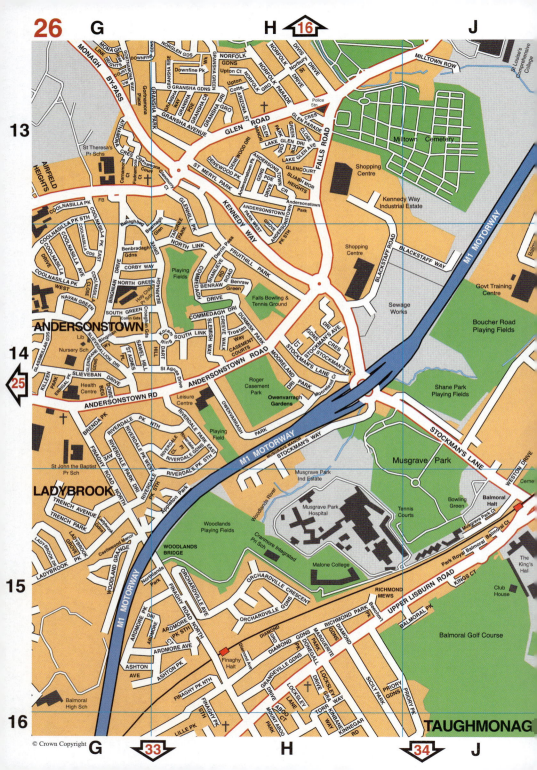

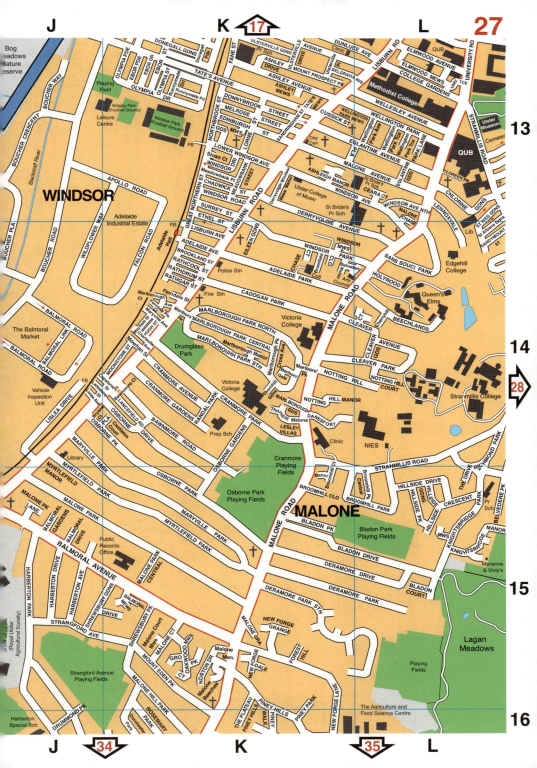

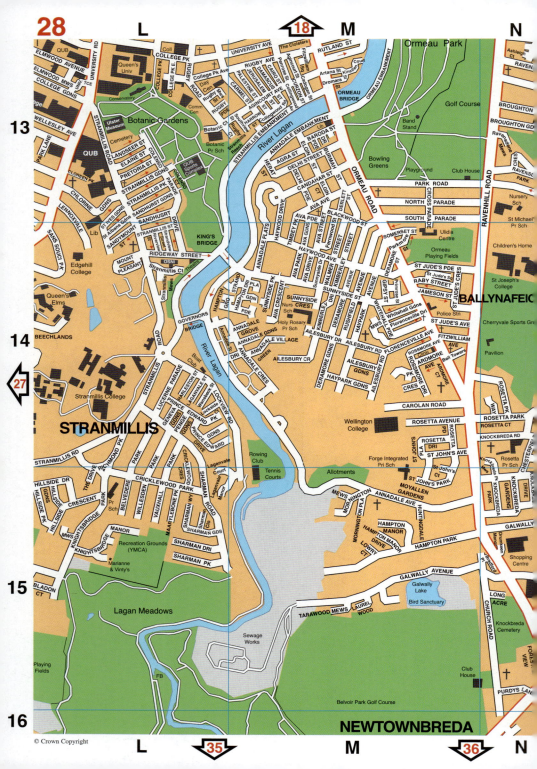

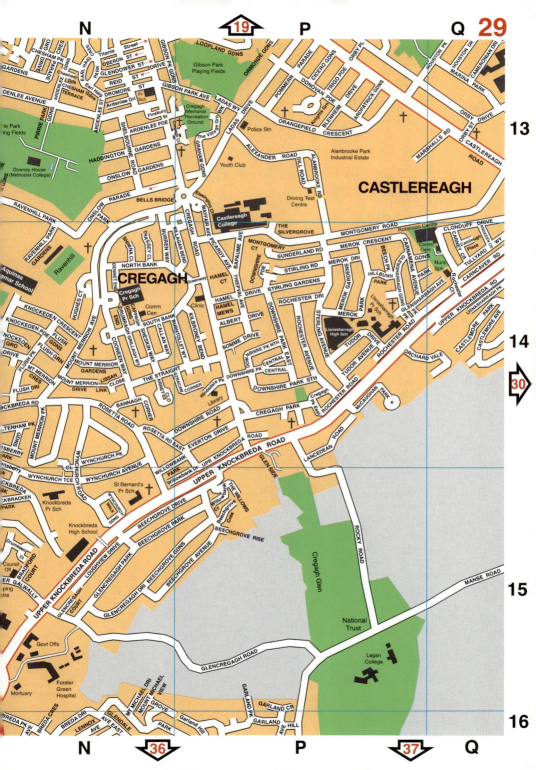

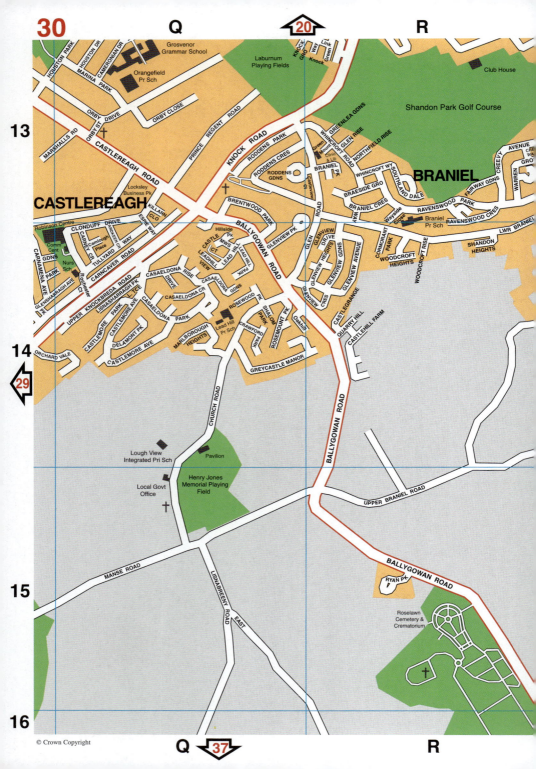

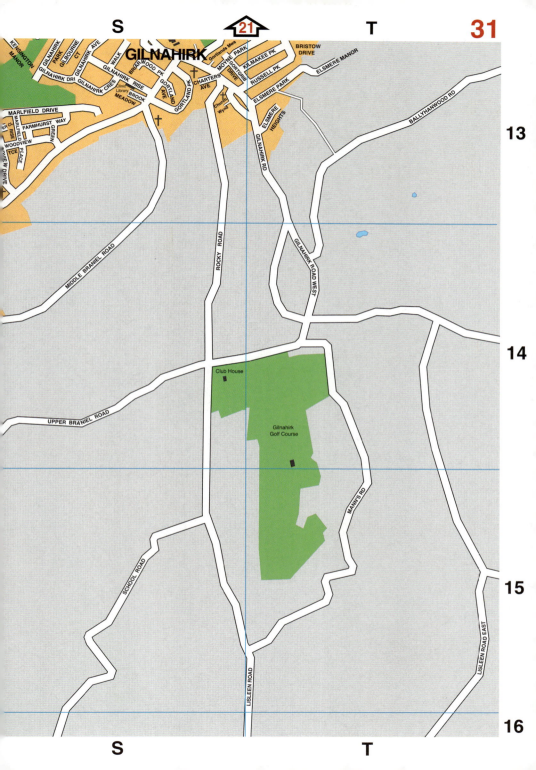

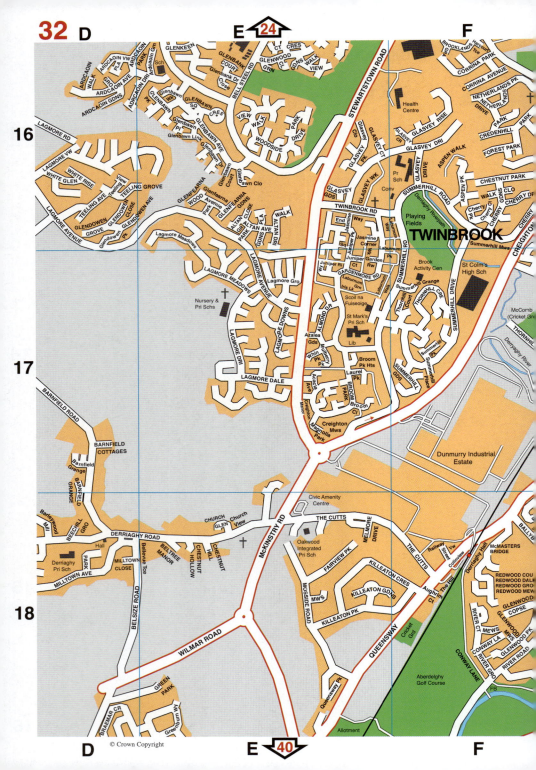

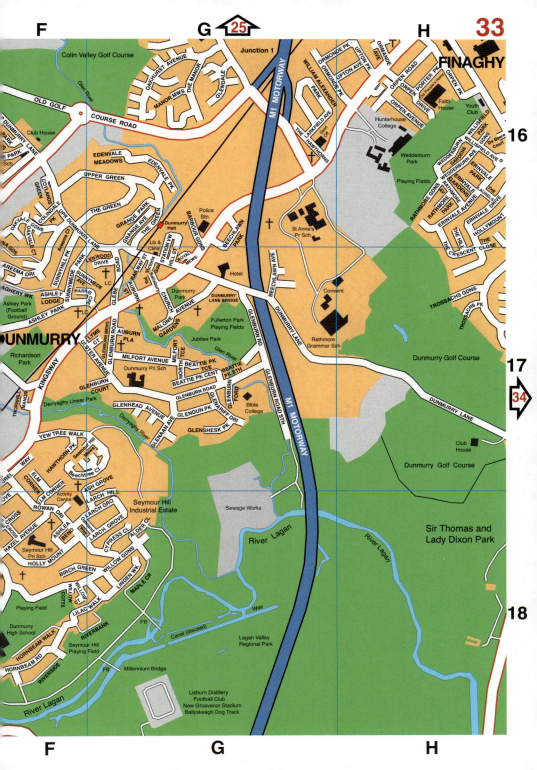

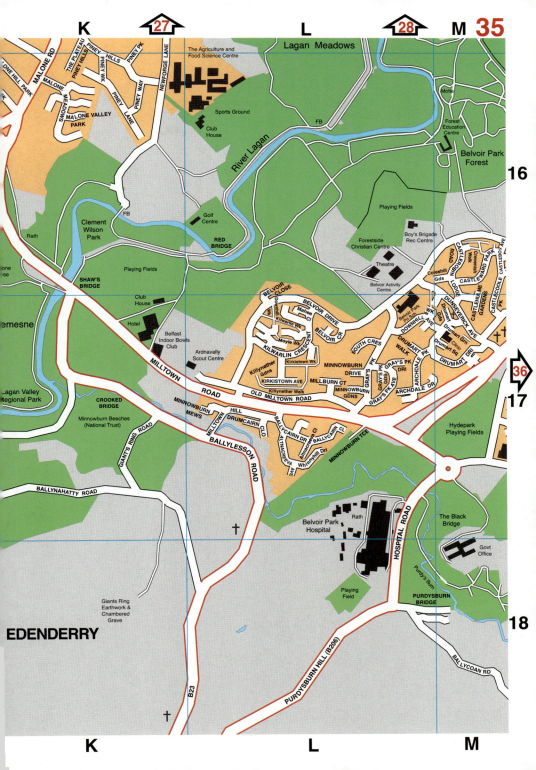

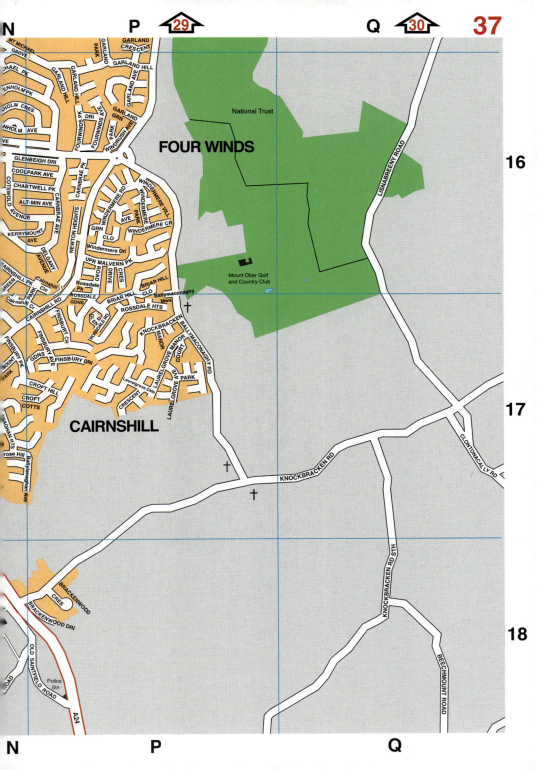

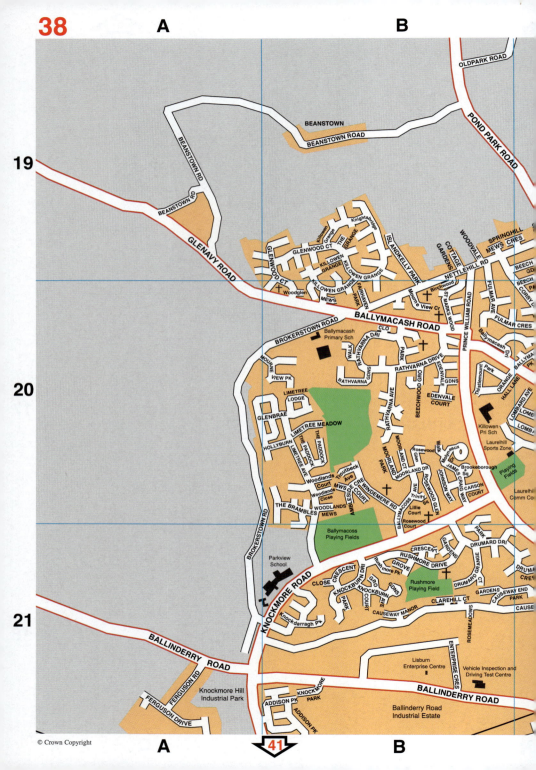

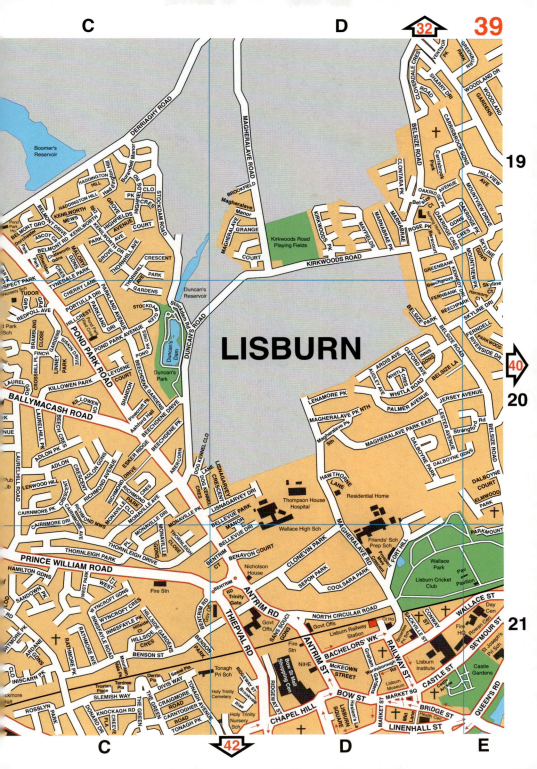

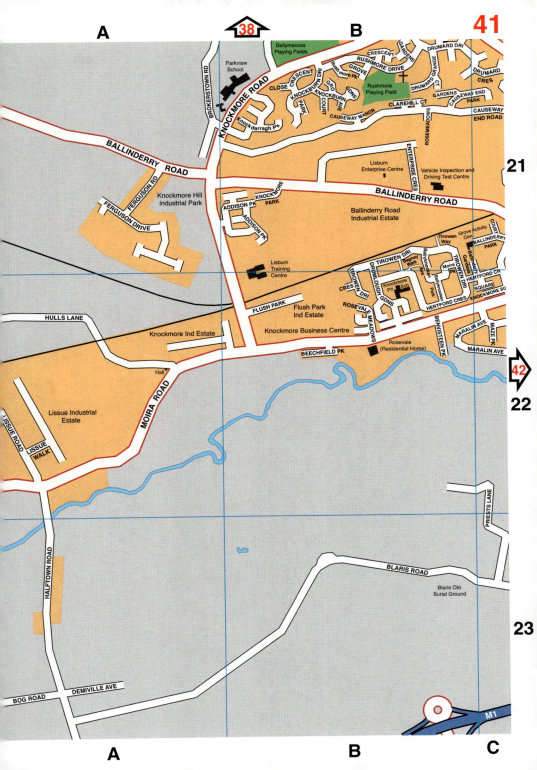

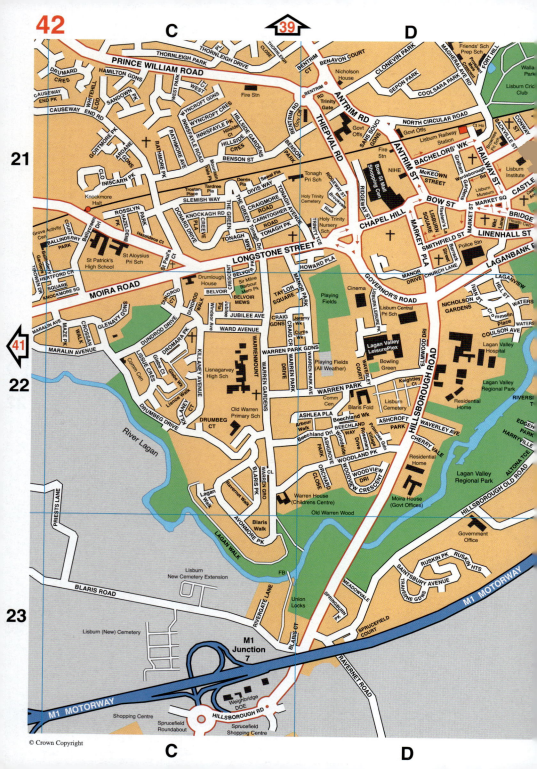

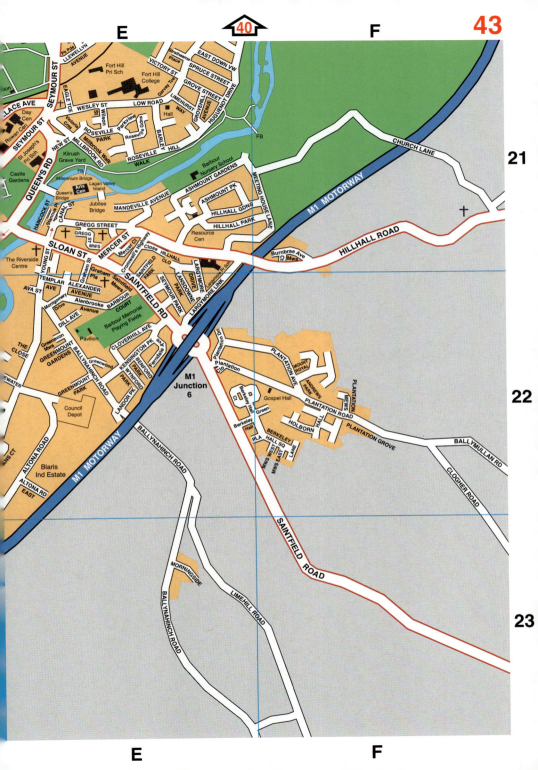

STREET INDEX

Due to insufficient space, some streets and/or their names have been omitted from the street map. Street names below which are prefixed by a * are not represented on the map, but they can be located by referring in the index to the name of the street which follows in brackets.

Page		Grid Ref	Page		Grid Ref	Page		Grid Ref	Page		Grid Ref
3	A8(M) Motorway	H2	17	Agnes Street	K10	42	Altona Terrace	D22	7	Ardeen Avenue	M4
5	Abbey Court	N3	28	Agra Street	M13	38	Ambleside Court	B20	7	Ardeen Gardens	M4
7	Abbey Crescent	M4	19	Aigburth Park	P11	17	Ambleside Court	K10	29	Ardenlee Avenue	N13
21	Abbey Court	T12	28	Ailesbury Crescent	M14	38	Ambleside Crescent	B20	18	Ardenlee Close	N13
10	Abbey Dale Crescent	H9	28	Ailesbury Drive	M14	38	Ambleside Mews	B20	19	Ardenlee Crescent	N13
10	Abbey Dale Court	J9	28	Ailesbury Gardens	M14	17	Ambleside Street	K10	18	Ardenlee Court	N13
10	Abbey Dale Drive	H9	28	Ailesbury Road	M14	16	Amcomri Street	J11	29	Ardenlee Drive	N13
10	Abbey Dale Garden	H9	28	Ailesbury Road	M14	18	Amelia Street	L12	29	Ardenlee Gardens	N13
10	Abbey Dale Parade	H9	17	Ainsworth Avenue	J11	18	Ampere Street	N12	18	Ardenlee Green	N13
10	Abbey Dale Park	H9	17	Ainsworth Drive	J11	18	Anderson Court	N11	29	Ardenlee Parade	N13
21	Abbey Gardens	S12	17	Ainsworth Pass	J11		(Cuirt Andarsan)		19	Ardenlee Park	N13
4	Abbey Green	M1	17	Ainsworth Parade	J10	25	Andersonstown Cres	H13	19	Ardenlee Place	N13
7	Abbey Park	M4	17	Ainsworth Street	J11		(Corran Bhaile Andarsan)		18	Ardenlee Rise	N13
21	Abbey Park	S12	25	Airfield Heights	G13	25	Andersonstown Drive	H13	29	Ardenlee Street	N13
44	Abbey Place	S7	13	Airport Road	P9	25	Andersonstown Gdns	H13	19	Ardenlee Way	N13
44	Abbey Ring	S7	14	Airport Road West	Q8	25	Andersonstown Grove	H14	19	Ardenvohr Street	N12
21	Abbey Road	S12	43	Alanbrooke Avenue	E22	25	Andersonstown Pde	H13	19	Ardenwood	N13
5	Abbeycroft Drive	N2	29	Alanbrooke Road	P13	25	Andersonstown Park	H13	7	Ardfarn Close	M4
5	Abbeycroft Gardens	N2	17	Albany Place	K11		(Pairc Bhaile Andarsan)		7	Ardgart Place	M4
5	Abbeycroft Road	N2	17	Albany Square	K11	25	Andersonstown Park	H13	19	Ardgowan Drive	P12
7	Abbeydale Close	N4	18	Albert Bridge	M12		(Pairc Bhaile Andarsan)		19	Ardgowan Street	N12
7	Abbeydene Manor	N4	17	Albert Court	L11	25	Andersonstown Pk Sth	H14	20	Ardgreenan Crescent	R11
5	Abbeyglen Crescent	N2	29	Albert Drive	P14	25	Andersonstown Pk West	H13	20	Ardgreenan Drive	R11
5	Abbeyglen Park	N2	18	Albert Square	M11	25	Andersonstown Road	H14	20	Ardgreenan Gardens	R11
5	Abbeyhill Drive	M2	17	Albert Street	K11		(Bothar Bhaile Andarsan)		20	Ardgreenan Mount	R11
5	Abbeyhill Gardens	M2	17	Albert Street	L11	43	Andrews Park	F22	20	Ardgreenan Place	R11
5	Abbeyhill Park	M2	19	Albertbridge Road	N12	18	Ann Street	M11	11	Ardilea Court	K10
5	Abbeyhill Road	M2	11	Albertville Drive	K10	28	Annadale Avenue	M15	11	Ardilea Drive	K9
5	Abbeyhill Way	M2	18	Albion Lane	L12	28	Annadale Crescent	M14	11	Ardilea Street	K10
5	Abbeytown Square	M1	17	Albion Street	L12	28	Annadale Drive	M14	39	Ardis Avenue	D20
5	Abbeyville Gardens	N3	33	Alder Close	G18	28	Annadale Embankment	M13	30	Ardkeen Crescent	Q14
5	Abbeyville Park	N3	31	Alder Close	S18	28	Annadale Flats	M14	7	Ardlea Crescent	M4
5	Abbeyville Place	N3	36	Alderwood Close	M17	28	Annadale Gardens	M14	44	Ardlee Avenue	S7
5	Abbeyville Street	N3	36	Alderwood Hill	M17	28	Annadale Green	M14	7	Ardmillan Drive	M4
5	Abbots Cross	M3	43	Alexander Avenue	E22	28	Annadale Grove	M14	11	Ardmillan	L8
5	Abbots Drive	M3	29	Alexander Road	P13	28	Annadale Terrace	L14	7	Ardmillan Gardens	M4
5	Abbots Gardens	M3	11	Alexandra Avenue	L9	28	Annadale Village	M14	16	Ardmonagh Gardens	H12
5	Abbots Road	M3	11	Alexandra Gardens	L8	11	Annalee Court	K10	16	Ardmonagh Parade	G12
44	Abbots Wood	S7	44	Alexandra Park	S7	17	Annesley Street	L10	16	Ardmonagh Way	H12
7	Abbotscoole House	M4	12	Alexandra Park Ave	L9	17	Annsboro Street	K11	25	Ardmore Avenue	M15
39	Abercorn	C20	44	Alexandra Place	S6	11	*Antigua Court	K10	28	Ardmore Avenue	M14
17	Abercorn Street	L13	21	Alford Park	T12		(Antigua Street)		44	Ardmore Avenue	T7
17	Abercorn Street Nth	K12	18	Alfred Street	M12	11	Antigua Street	K10	23	Ardmore Avenue	W12
17	Abercorn Walk	K12	33	Alina Gardens	F16	6	Antrim Road	K4	23	Ardmore Avenue	W12
17	Aberdeen Street	K11	11	Alliance Avenue	J9	9	Antrim Road	L7	25	Ardmore Court	H15
40	Aberdelghy Gardens	E19	11	Alliance Close	J9	11	Antrim Road	L10	28	Ardmore Court	M14
40	Aberdelghy Grove	E19	11	Alliance Crescent	J9	42	Antrim Road	D21	25	Ardmore Drive	G15
40	Aberdelghy Park	E19	11	Alliance Drive	J9	42	Antrim Street	D21	44	Ardmore Heights	T7
34	Aberfoyle Gardens	H17	11	Alliance Gardens	J9	27	Apollo Road	K13	25	Ardmore Park	G15
34	Aberfoyle Park	H17	11	Alliance Green	J9	25	Appleton Park	H15	25	Ardmore Park South	H15
3	Abernethy Drive	K2	11	Alliance Parade	J9	18	Apsley Street	L12	44	Ardmore Park	T6
3	Abernethy Gardens	K2	11	Alliance Park	J9	11	Arbour Street	K9	44	Ardmore Road	T7
3	Abernethy Park	K2	10	Alliance Road	J9	42	Arbour Walk	D22	44	Ardmore Terrace	T6
19	Abetta Parade	P12	11	Alloa Street	K10	35	Archdale Drive	L17	17	Ardmoulin Avenue	K11
17	Abingdon Drive	K12	11	Allworthy Avenue	L9	35	Archdale Park	L17	17	Ardmoulin Close	K11
25	Aboo Court	H15	32	Almond Drive	E17	3	Archvale Avenue	K3	17	Ardmoulin Place	K11
17	Abyssinia Street	K12	40	Alpha Court	E20	3	Archvale Crescent	K3	17	Ardmoulin Street	K11
17	Abyssinia Walk	K12	40	Alpha Mews	E20	3	Archvale Gardens	K3	17	Ardmoulin Terrace	K11
32	Acacia Avenue	E17	32	Altan Avenue	E16	3	Archvale Park	K3	17	Ardnaclowney Drive	J12
17	Academy Street	L11	32	Altan Close	E16	22	Ardara Avenue	U12	44	Ardnagreena Gardens	S7
17	Acton Street	K10	32	Altan Drive	E16	22	Ardara Mews	U12	16	Ard-Na-Va Road	J12
4	Adare Park	M1	32	Altan Gardens	E16	42	Ardane Gardens	C21	23	Ardnoe Avenue	V12
41	Addison Park	B21	32	Altan Grove	E16	12	Ardavon Park	L8	11	Ardoyne Avenue	K9
11	Adela Place	L10	32	Altan Park	E16	32	Ardcaoin Avenue	D16	11	Ardoyne Court	K9
11	Adela Street	L10	32	Altan Walk	E16	32	Ardcaoin Drive	D16	11	Ardoyne Place	K9
27	Adelaide Avenue	K14	18	Altcar Court	N11	32	Ardcaoin Gardens	D16	10	Ardoyne Road	J9
27	Adelaide Chase	K14		(Cuirt Alt an Chairthe)		32	Ardcaoin Green	E16	11	Ardoyne Walk	K9
27	Adelaide Park	K14	37	Alt-Min Avenue	N16	32	Ardcaoin Grove	D16	29	Ardpatrick Gardens	P13
18	Adelaide Street	L12	7	Altmore Green	M4	32	Ardcaoin Park	D16	4	Ardrannay Drive	M2
22	Adlon Crescent	C20	35	Altnacreeva Avenue	L17	32	Ardcaoin Place	D16	5	Ards Drive	N2
22	Adlon Gardens	C20	35	Altnacreeva Close	L17	32	Ardcaoin View	D16	5	Ards Park	N1
39	Adlon Park	C20	4	Altncreeve Park	M3	32	Ardcaoin Walk	D16	5	Ardtole Park	N2
16	Advantage Way	H11	25	Altnamona Crescent	G13	21	Ardcarn Drive	T12	20	Ardvarna Crescent	R10
33	Aghery Walk	F17	18	Alton Street	L11	21	Ardcarn Green	T12	20	Ardvarna Park	R10
28	Agincourt Avenue	M13		(Sraid Loch Altain)		21	Ardcarn Park	T12	33	Areema Court	F16
28	Agincourt Street	M13	43	Altona Road	E22	21	Ardcarn Way	T12	33	Areema Drive	F17
17	Agnes Close	K10	43	Altona Road East	E22	7	Ardcloon Avenue	M4	17	Argyle Court	K11
									17	Argyle Street	K11

STREET INDEX

Page	Street	Grid Ref	Page	Street	Grid Ref	Page	Street	Grid Ref	Page	Street	Grid Ref
17	Argyle Street	K11	28	Ava Crescent	M14	3	Ballyhenry Gardens	H2	21	Barnett's Court	S12
17	Ariel Street	M14	28	Ava Drive	M14	3	Ballyhenry Grove	J2	21	Barnett's Court Mews	S12
25	Arizona Street	H13	28	Ava Gardens	M14	3	Ballyhenry Parade	H2	21	Barnett's Crescent	S12
25	Arlington Drive	G15	28	Ava Park	M14	3	Ballyhenry Park	H2	21	Barnett's Green	S12
25	Arlington Park	G15	28	Ava Parade	M13	3	Ballyhenry Road	H2	21	Barnett's Lodge	S12
17	Armitage Close	P11	28	Ava Street	M14	41	Ballyknockan Avenue	B21	21	Barnett's Road	S12
7	Armoy Gardens	M4	43	Ava Street	E22	41	Ballyknockan Park	B22	32	Barnfield Cottages	D17
29	Arney Close	N14	16	Avoca Close	G12	37	Ballylenaghan Avenue	N17	32	Barnfield Grange	D17
17	Arnon Street	N11	11	Avoca Street	K10	37	Ballylenaghan Heights	N17	32	Barnfield Grange	D17
	(Sraid Earnain)		11	Avonbeg Close	K10	37	Ballylenaghan Park	N17	32	Barnfield Road	D17
12	Arosa Parade	M9	19	Avondale Street	P12	36	Ballylenaghan Road	N17	28	Baroda Drive	M13
18	Arran Court	N11	19	Avoniel Drive	P12	35	Ballylesson Road	L17	28	Baroda Parade	M13
23	Arran Park	W12	19	Avoniel Parade	P12	19	Ballymacarrett Road	N11	28	Baroda Street	M13
18	Arran Street	N11	19	Avoniel Road	N12	19	Ballymacarrett Walkway	P11	42	Barrack Street	D21
	(Sraid Arann)		7	Avonlea Gardens	M4	38	Ballymacash Drive	B20	17	Barrack Street	L11
28	Artana Street	M13	42	Avonmore Park	C23	38	Ballymacash Park	C20	17	Barrington Gardens	K12
7	Arthur Avenue	L5	19	Avonorr Drive	P12	38	Ballymacash Road	B10	39	Bascourt	D19
7	Arthur Crescent	L5	14	Avonvale	R10	37	Ballymaconaghy Mews	P17	19	Baskin Street	N11
18	Arthur Lane	M11	12	Ayr Street	M9	37	Ballymaconaghy Road	P17	20	Bathgate Drive	Q11
7	Arthur Park	L5	32	Azalea Gardens	E17	38	Ballymenoch Avenue	B20	19	Batley Street	P12
18	Arthur Place	L11	17	Azamor Street	K11	16	Ballymagarry Lane	H11	17	Battenberg Street	J11
7	Arthur Road	L5				11	*Ballymena Court	K10	27	Bawnmore Court	K14
18	*Arthur Square	L11					(Ballymoney Street)		7	Bawnmore Grove	M5
	(Arthur Street)		42	BACHELOR'S WALK	D21	44	Ballymenoch Park	T6	7	Bawnmore Park	M5
18	Arthur Street	L11	17	Bainesmore Drive	J11	15	Ballymiscaw Road	T10	7	Bawnmore Place	M5
17	Arundel Courts	K12	18	Bains Place	L12	11	Ballymoney Street	K10	27	Bawnmore Road	K14
17	*Arundel Walk	K12	18	Balfour Avenue	M13	43	Ballymullan Road	F22	7	Bawnmore Terrace	M5
	(Arundel Courts)		10	Balholm Drive	J10	16	Ballymurphy Crescent	H12	38	Beanstown Road	A19
39	Ascot Crescent	C19	17	Balkan Court	K11	16	Ballymurphy Drive	H12	25	Bearnagh Drive	H14
20	Ascot Gardens	R13	17	Balkan Street	K11	16	Ballymurphy Parade	H12	25	Bearnagh Glen	H14
20	Ascot Mews	R13	25	Ballaghbeg	G13	16	Ballymurphy Road	H12	33	Beattie Park Central	G17
20	Ascot Park	R13	18	Ballarat Court	M12	16	Ballymurphy Road	H12	33	Beattie Park North	G17
44	Ash Gardens	S7	18	Ballarat Street	M12	17	Ballymurphy Street	J12	33	Beattie Park South	G17
33	Ash Grove	G17	41	Ballinderry Court	C21	35	Ballynahatty Road	K17	33	Beattie Park Terrace	G17
3	Ashbourne	K2	41	Ballinderry Gardens	B21	43	Ballynahinch Road	E22	36	Beaufort Avenue	M16
40	Ashbourne Park	E19	41	Ballinderry Park	C21	2	Ballynure Road	H1	36	Beaufort Crescent	M16
14	Ashbrook Crescent	Q10	41	Ballinderry Road	B21	11	Ballynure Street	K9	36	Beaufort Gardens	M16
14	Ashbrook Drive	Q10	4	Ballyalton Park	M1	11	*Ballynure Way	K9	36	Beaufort Grove	M16
20	Ashburn Green	R10	5	Ballyalton Walk	M1		(Ballynure Street)		36	Beaufort Park	N16
18	Ashburne Mews	L12	23	Ballybeen Park	V12	23	Ballyoran Lane	W11	23	Beauly Drive	W12
18	Ashburne Place	L12	23	Ballybeen Square	V12	22	Ballyregan Avenue	U11	18	Bedford Street	L12
42	Ashcroft Park	D22	32	Ballybog Road	F18	23	Ballyregan Crescent	V11	39	Beech Crescent	C20
19	Ashdale Street	P11	35	Ballycairn Close	L17	23	Ballyregan Drive	V11	44	Beech End	S7
11	Ashdene Drive	L9	35	Ballycairn Drive	L17	23	Ballyregan Park	V11	38	Beech Hill Gardens	C19
11	Ashfield Crescent	L9	11	Ballycarry Street	K9	22	Ballyregan Road	U11	38	Beech Hill Park	C20
11	Ashfield Court	L9	11	Ballycastle Court	K10	22	Ballyregan Road	U11	32	Beech Grove	F18
11	Ashfield Drive	L9	11	Ballyclare Court	K9	7	Ballyronan Park	M4	29	Beech Park	P14
12	Ashfield Gardens	L9	3	Ballyclare Road	J2	7	Ballyronny Hill	L5	39	Beechdene Drive	C20
20	Ashford Green	R10	3	Ballyclare Road	H1	10	Ballysillan Avenue	H8	39	Beechdene Gardens	C20
39	Ashford Hall	C20	11	Ballyclare Street	K10	10	Ballysillan Crescent	J8	39	Beechdene Park	C20
11	Ashford Lodge	J1	11	Ballyclare Way	K10	10	Ballysillan Drive	J8	19	Beechfield Court	N11
11	Ashgrove Park	K9	35	Ballycoan Road	M18	10	Ballysillan Park	J8	41	Beechfield Park	B22
42	Ashgrove Park	D22	3	Ballycraigy Gardens	J1	10	Ballysillan Road	J8	19	Beechfield Street	N11
3	Ashgrove Road	K3	3	Ballycraigy Park	J1	40	Ballyskeagh Road	F19		(Sraid Phairc na Fea)	
33	Ashlea Bend	H1	2	Ballycraigy Road	H1	3	Ballyvesey Court	J1	19	Beechfield Street	N11
42	Ashlea Place	D22	2	Ballycraigy Road South	F1	2	Ballyvesey Green	G1	39	Beechgrove	D20
28	Ashleigh Court	N13	3	Ballycraigy Way	J1	3	Ballyvesey Park	J1	29	Beechgrove Avenue	P15
27	Ashleigh Manor	K13	42	Ballycreen Drive	C21	3	Ballyvesey Rise	J1	29	Beechgrove Crescent	P15
17	Ashley Avenue	K13	4	Ballyduff Brae	L1	2	Ballyvesey Road	G1	3	Beechgrove Crescent	K1
17	Ashley Drive	K13	4	Ballyduff Close	L1	4	Balmoral Avenue	J15	3	Beechgrove Drive	K1
9	Ashley Gardens	HL7	4	Ballyduff Gardens	L1	26	Balmoral Court	J15	29	Beechgrove Drive	N15
33	Ashley Lodge	F17	4	Ballyduff Road	L2	27	Balmoral Drive	J15	3	Beechgrove Gardens	K1
27	Ashley Mews	K13	4	Ballyduff Walk	L1	27	Balmoral Gardens	J15	29	Beechgrove Gardens	N15
33	Ashley Park	F17	3	Ballyearl Close	J1	27	Balmoral Link	J14	29	Beechgrove Park	N15
17	Ashmore Place	K11	3	Ballyearl Court	J1	27	Balmoral Mews	K15	29	Beechgrove Rise	P15
17	Ashmore Street	K11	3	Ballyearl Crescent	J1	26	Balmoral Park	J15	36	Beechill Avenue	N17
43	Ashmount Gardens	E21	3	Ballyearl Drive	J1	27	Balmoral Road	J14	36	Beechill Court	N17
20	Ashmount Grove	R10	3	Ballyearl Green	J1	11	Baltic Avenue	L9	32	Beechill Grove	D18
20	Ashmount Park	R10	3	Ballyearl Rise	J1	19	Banbury Street	P11	36	Beechill Park	N1
43	Ashmount Park	E21	3	Ballyearl Terrace	J1	11	Bandon Court	K10	36	Beechill Park Avenue	N17
25	Ashton Avenue	G15	3	Ballyearl Way	J1	23	Banff Park	V12	36	Beechill Park East	N16
25	Ashton Park	H15	4	Ballyfore Avenue	L1	23	Banff Walk	V12	36	Beechill Park North	N16
4	Aspen Park	F16	4	Ballyfore Gardens	L1	44	Bangor Road	T6	36	Beechill Park West	N16
4	Aspen Park	M2	4	Ballyfore Park	L1	18	Bank Street	L11	36	Beechill Park South	N17
4	Aspen Walk	F16	4	Ballyfore Parade	L1	18	Bankmore Street	L12	36	Beechill Road	N17
20	Aston Gardens	R11	4	Ballyfore Road	L1	29	Bann Court	K10	42	Beechland Drive	D22
20	Astoria Gardens	R12	4	Ballyfore Walk	L1	29	Bannagh Corner	N14	42	Beechland Walk	D22
20	Astoria Gardens	R12	16	Ballygomartin Drive	H11	17	Bantry Street	J11	42	Beechland Way	D22
17	Athol Street	L12	16	Ballygomartin Park	J10	29	Bapaume Avenue	P14	27	Beechlands	L14
17	Athol Street Lane	L12	10	Ballygomartin Road	J10	43	Barbour Court	E22	33	Beechlawn Avenue	G17
11	Atlantic Avenue	L9	16	Ballygomartin Road	H11	33	Barbour Gardens	G16	33	Beechlawn Park	G16
20	Auburn Place	G17	8	Ballygowan Road	R14	40	Barbour Lodge	E20	17	Beechmount Avenue	J12
33	Auburn Street	G17	31	Ballyhanwood Road	T13	43	Barley Hill	E21	17	Beechmount Close	J12
4	Audley Avenue	D20	22	Ballyhanwood Road	U13	32	Barleymond Mill	D18	17	Beechmount Crescent	J12
32	Aughrim Court	F18	3	Ballyhenry Avenue	H2	7	Barna Square	M4	17	Beechmount Drive	J12
17	Aughrim Park	L12	3	Ballyhenry Crescent	J2	12	Barnett Dock Road	M10	17	Beechmount Gardens	J12
28	Ava Avenue	M13	3	Ballyhenry Drive	H2	21	Barnett's Chase	S12	17	Beechmount Grove	J12

STREET INDEX

Page		Grid Ref	Page		Grid Ref	Page		Grid Ref	Page		Grid Ref
16	Beechmount Parade	J11	17	Benares Street	J11	27	Bladon Drive	K15	17	Bread Street	K11
26	Beechmount Park	H15	42	Benavon Court	D21	27	Bladon Park	K15	19	Breach Close	N12
17	Beechmount Pass	J12	25	Benbradagh Gardens	G14	17	Blaney Street	K10	36	Breda Avenue	N16
37	Beechmount Road	Q18	17	Benburb Street	K13	42	Blaris Court	C23	36	Breda Crescent	N16
17	Beechmount Street	J12	7	Bencrom Park	M4	42	Blaris Park	C22	36	Breda Drive	N16
11	Beechnut Park	K10	18	Bendigo Street	M12	41	Blaris Road	B23	36	Breda Gardens	N16
39	Beechpark	D20	43	Benford Park	E22	42	Blaris Walk	C23	36	Breda Parade	N16
11	Beechpark Street	K10	34	Benmore Court	H16	10	Bleach Green	H8	36	Breda Park	N16
33	Beechtree Court	F17	34	Benmore Drive	H16	5	Bleach Green Avenue	M2	36	Breda Road	N16
16	Beechview Park	J12	34	Benmore Drive	H16	5	Bleach Green Court	M2	36	Breda Terrace	N16
44	Beechwood	T6	34	Benmore Walk	H16	16	Bleach Green Terrace	J12	25	Brenda Park	G14
7	Beechwood Avenue	M4	23	Bennan Park	B12	29	Blenheim Drive	P13	19	Brenda Street	P12
36	Beechwood Court	M17	11	Bennett Drive	K9	19	Blondin Street	L12	30	Brentwood Park	Q13
38	Beechwood Grove	B20	25	Benraw Green	H14	19	Bloomdale Street	P11	36	Brerton Crescent	M17
36	Beechwood Grove	M17	25	Benraw Road	H14	19	Bloomfield Avenue	P11	36	Brerton Grove	M17
22	Beechwood Manor	U12	42	Benson Park	C21	19	Bloomfield Court	P12	24	Brian's Well Close	E15
19	Beechwood Street	P11	42	Benson Street	C21	19	Bloomfield Crescent	P12	24	Brian's Well Court	E15
19	Beersbridge Road	P12	17	Bentham Drive	K12	19	Bloomfield Drive	P12	24	Brian's Well Road	E15
41	Begney Walk	B21	12	Bentinck Street	M10	19	Bloomfield Gardens	P12	8	Brianville Park	K7
17	Beit Street	K12	42	Bentrim Court	D21	19	Bloomfield Park	P12	37	Briar Hill	P17
17	Belair Street	J11	42	Bentrim Road	C21	19	Bloomfield Park West	P12	37	Briar Hill Close	P16
40	Belfast Road	E20	10	Benview Avenue	J8	19	Bloomfield Parade	P12	31	Briarwood Park	S13
2	Belfast Road	G3	10	Benview Drive	J8	19	Bloomfield Road	P12	21	Briarwood Views	S13
14	Belfast Road	R8	10	Benview Park	J8	19	Bloomfield Street	P12	18	Brickhill Park	J1
23	Belfast Road	W11	10	Benview Parade	J8	19	Bloomfield Walkway	P11	18	Bridge End	M11
16	Belfield Heights	G12	41	Benvisteen Park	B22	17	Blythe Street	L12	4	Bridge Road	L1
7	Belfry View	M4	25	Benwee Park	F15	41	Bog Road	A23	42	Bridge Street	D21
17	Belgrave Street	K11	43	Berkeley Hall	E22	17	Bombay Street	K11	40	Bridge Street	E20
27	Belgravia Avenue	K13	43	Berkeley Hall Court	E22	10	Boodles Hill	H8	18	Bridge Street	L11
17	Bell Close	K10	43	Berkeley Hall Green	E22	10	Boodles Lane	H8	19	Bright Street	N11
28	Bell Towers	M14	43	Berkeley Hall Lane	F22	17	Bootle Street	K10	17	Brighton Street	L12
32	Bell Steel Road	E16	43	Berkeley Hall Mews East	F22	18	Botanic Avenue	L12	9	Bristol Avenue	L7
18	Bellbashford Court	N12	43	Berkeley Hall Mews West	F22	19	Botanic Court	L13	21	Bristow Drive	T13
6	Bellevue Drive	L4	43	Berkeley Hall Place	F22	27	Boucher Crescent	J13	34	Bristow Park	J16
39	Bellevue Drive	D21	43	Berkeley Hall Square	F22	27	Boucher Place	J14	17	Britannic Drive	L12
39	Bellevue Manor	D20	12	Berkeley Road	M10	27	Boucher Road	J14	17	Britannic Park	L12
6	Bellevue Manor	K4	36	Berkley Court	M16	27	Boucher Way	J13	17	Britannic Terrace	L12
39	Bellevue Park	D20	17	Berlin Street	K11	17	Boundary Street	L11	16	Britton's Drive	H12
6	Bellevue Park	L4	18	Berry Street	L11	17	Boundary Walk	L11	16	Britton's Court	H12
17	Bellevue Street	K11	11	Berwick Road	J9	17	Boundary Way	L11	17	Britton's Parade	J12
32	Bellevue Tce	E18	36	Bests' Hill Court	M17	42	Bow Street	D12	17	Broadway	J12
40	Bell's Lane Park	E19	36	Bests' Hill Glen	M17	17	Bowness Street	K10	17	Broadway	K13
29	Bells Bridge	N13	36	Bests' Hill Lane	M17	17	Boyd Street	L11	17	Broadway Court	J12
40	Bells Lane	E19	36	Bests' Hill View	M17	17	Boyne Court	L12	17	Broadway Parade	K13
20	Belmont Avenue	R11	20	Bethany Street	Q11	7	Bracken Drive	M4	23	Brodick Way	W12
20	Belmont Avenue West	Q11	3	Beverley Avenue	K1	7	Bracken Way	M4	41	Brokerstown Road	A21
20	Belmont Church Road	Q11	3	Beverley Crescent	K1	4	Brackens Court	K2	38	Brokerstown Road	B20
20	Belmont Close	Q11	3	Beverley Drive	K1	37	Brackenwood Crescent	P18	27	Bromfield	K14
20	Belmont Court	Q11	3	Beverley Gardens	K1	37	Brackenwood Drive	P18	17	Bromley Street	K10
20	Belmont Drive	R11	3	Beverley Grove	K1	34	Brackenwood Lane	J17	11	Brompton Park	J10
39	Belmont Drive	C19	3	Beverley Park	K2	7	Bradan Heights	L4	31	Brook Meadow	S13
20	Belmont Grange	Q11	3	Beverley Road	K1	18	Bradbury Place	L12	44	Brook Street	T6
39	Belmont Grove	C19	17	Beverley Street	K11	29	Bradford Court	N15	25	Brooke Close	G15
20	Belmont Mews	Q11	10	Bilston Road	H9	28	Bradford Place	N15	25	Brooke Court	G15
20	Belmont Park	Q11	25	Bingnian Drive	G14	18	*Bradford Square	M11	25	Brooke Crescent	G15
20	Belmont Place	R11	25	Bingnian Way	G14		(Steam Mill Lane)		25	Brooke Drive	G15
39	Belmont Road	C19	3	Birch Dale	H2	17	*Brady's Lane	L11	25	Brooke Drive	G15
20	Belmont Road	R11	44	Birch Drive	T6		(Boundary Street)		25	Brooke Manor	G15
20	Belmont Road	Q11	3	Birch Green	H2	10	Brae Hill Crescent	H8	25	Brooke Park	G15
21	Belmont Road	S10	33	Birch Green	F18	10	Brae Hill Link	H8	25	Brooke Park	G15
18	Belmore Street	M13	3	Birch Lane	H2	10	Brae Hill Park	H8	38	Brookeborough Square	B20
7	Belmore Gardens	M4	3	Birch Meadow	H2	10	Brae Hill Parade	H8	39	Brookfield	D19
39	Belsize Court	D19	3	Birch View	H2	10	Brae Hill Road	H8	11	Brookfield Place	J10
32	Belsize Lane	D20	3	Birchmount	K1	10	Brae Hill Way	H8	11	Brookfield Street	J10
32	Belsize Park	D20	38	Birchwood	B20	3	Braemar Court	J3	11	Brookfield Walk	J10
39	Belsize Road	D20	2	Birmingham Road	G3	3	Braemar Court	J3	11	Brookhill Avenue	L9
32	Belsize Road	D18	16	Black Mountain Grove	H11	32	Braemar Crescent	D18	27	Brookland Street	K14
6	Bellevue Park	L4	16	Black Mountain Parade	H11	17	Braemar Street	J12	23	Brooklands Avenue	V11
32	Beltree Manor	E18	16	Black Mountain Park	H11	4	Braeside Avenue	L1	23	Brooklands Crescent	V11
27	Belvedere Manor	K14	16	Black Mountain Place	H11	4	Braeside Drive	L1	23	Brooklands Drive	V12
27	Belvedere Park	L15	16	Black Mountain Walk	H11	30	Braeside Grove	R13	23	Brooklands Gardens	V12
35	Belvoir Close	L16	16	Black Mountain Way	H11	4	Braeside Park	L1	32	Brooklands Grange	F16
42	Belvoir Crescent	C22	25	Black's Court	G15	3	Bramble Way	K1	23	Brooklands Park	V12
35	Belvoir Crescent	L17	25	Black's Road	G15	39	Brambling Close	C20	23	Brooklands Road	V12
35	Belvoir Drive	L17	25	Black's Mews	F15	19	Bramcote Street	P12	10	Brookmill Way	H8
42	Belvoir Mews	C22	26	Blackstaff Road	H14	19	Brandon Parade	P11	17	*Brookmount Gardens	J11
42	Belvoir Park	C22	26	Blackstaff Way	J14	19	Brandon Terrace	P11		(Centurion Street)	
36	Belvoir Road	M16	5	Blackthorn Drive	M1	19	Brandra Street	P11	17	Brookmount Street	K11
19	Belvoir Street	N11	5	Blackthorn Grange	M1	30	Braniel Crescent	R13	11	Brookvale Avenue	L9
36	Belvoir View Park	N16	5	Blackthorn Mews	M1	30	Braniel Park	R13	11	Brookvale Drive	L9
9	Ben Eden Avenue	L7	5	Blackthorn Road	M1	30	Braniel Way	R13	11	Brookvale Parade	K9
9	Ben Eden Court	L7	5	Blackthorn Road	L9	12	Brantwood Street	G9	42	Brookvale Rise	D21
9	Ben Eden Green	L7	5	Blackthorn Way	M1	17	Brassey Street	K12	11	Brookvale Street	K9
9	Ben Eden Park	L7	2	Blackwater Road	G1	11	Bray Close	J10	25	Brookville Court	L9
6	Ben Madigan Heights	L5	26	Blackwater Way	K12	11	Bray Court	J10	32	Broom Close	E17
6	Ben Madigan Park	L5	28	Blackwood Street	M13	11	Bray Street	J10	32	Broom Park	E17
6	Ben Madigan Park Sth	L5	27	Bladon Court	L15	11	Bray Street	J10	32	Broom Park Heights	E17

STREET INDEX

Page	Street	Grid Ref
17	Broom Street	J10
27	Broomhill Close	K15
27	Broomhill Court	K15
27	Broomhill Manor	K15
27	Broomhill Park	L15
27	Broomhill Park Central	L15
12	Brougham Street	M10
28	Broughton Gardens	N13
28	Broughton Park	N13
17	Brown Street	L11
44	Brown's Park	T6
18	Brown's Row	L11
17	Brown's Square	L11
18	Bruce Street	L12
11	Brucevale Court	L10
11	Brucevale Park	L10
18	Brunswick Street	L12
12	Brusleé Way	L10
17	Brussels Street	K10
27	Bryans Court	J14
19	Bryansford Place	N12
3	Bryson Court	J11
19	Bryson Court	N11
3	Bryson Gardens	J1
19	Bryson Gardens	N11
3	Bryson Park	J10
3	Bryson Square	J1
19	Bryson Street	N11
24	Bunbeg Park	F14
24	Buncrana Gardens	F14
19	Burandell Manor	C19
28	Burmah Street	M13
17	Burnaby Court	K12
17	Burnaby Park	K12
17	Burnaby Place	K12
17	Burnaby Walk	K12
17	Burnaby Way	K12
43	Burnbrae Avenue	F21
43	Burnbrae Court	F21
43	Burnbrae Mews	F21
3	Burney's Lane	J3
3	Burney's Mews	J3
2	Burnley Road	G3
36	Burnside Avenue	N16
36	Burnside Park	N16
3	Burnthill Avenue	J2
3	Burnthill Crescent	J2
3	Burnthill Drive	J2
3	Burnthill Gardens	J2
3	Burnthill Park	J2
3	Burnthill Road	J2
3	Burnthill Road	K2
29	Burntollet Way	P14
29	Burren Way	N14
18	Burton Avenue	V12
22	Burton Drive	U12
3	Bute Park	V12
12	Bute Street	JM9
11	Butler Place	J10
11	Butler Walk	J10
11	Butler Walk	J10
18	Buttermilk Loney	J8
44	Byron Place Mews	S6
21	CABIN HILL GDNS	S12
21	Cabin Hill Mews	S12
21	Cabin Hill Park	R12
21	Cabin Hill Court	R12
19	*Cable Close	N11
	(Scotch Row)	
27	Cadogan Park	K14
28	Cadogan Street	M13
14	Cairnburn Avenue	R10
14	Cairnburn Cresent	R10
20	Cairnburn Dell	R10
14	Cairnburn Drive	R10
14	Cairnburn Gardens	R10
20	Cairnburn Grange	R10
14	Cairnburn Park	R10
20	Cairnburn Road	R10
21	Cairnburn Road	S10
7	Cairncoole House	M4
10	Cairndale	H9
3	Cairngorm Crescent	J3
39	Cairnmore Avenue	C20
39	Cairnmore Crescent	C20

Page	Street	Grid Ref
39	Cairnmore Drive	C20
39	Cairnmore Park	C20
17	Cairns Street	K12
36	Cairnshill Avenue	N17
37	Cairnshill Close	P16
36	Cairnshill Court	N17
37	Cairnshill Crescent	N17
36	Cairnshill Drive	N16
37	Cairnshill Gardens	N16
37	Cairnshill Green	N16
37	Cairnshill Park	N16
37	Cairnshill Park	P16
36	Cairnshill Road	N17
23	Cairnsmore Avenue	W12
23	Cairnsmore Walk	V12
28	Cairo Street	M13
17	Caledon Court	J11
17	Caledon Street	J11
17	California Close	L11
29	Callan Way	N14
18	Callender Street	L11
19	Calvin Street	N12
11	Camberwell Court	L9
11	Camberwell Terrace	L9
34	Cambourne Park	K16
17	Cambrai Court	J10
5	Cambrai Drive	N3
5	Cambrai Park	N3
17	Cambrai Street	J10
23	Cambridge Manor	V12
12	*Cambridge Street	M10
	(Canning Street)	
17	Camden Street	L13
18	Cameron Street	L12
20	Cameronian Drive	Q13
30	Camlough Place	Q14
21	Campbell Chase	S11
20	Campbell Court	R11
20	Campbell Park Avenue	R11
3	Campbell Road	GK1
23	Campsie Park	W12
23	Campsie Park	V12
7	Camross Park	M4
19	Canada Street	N12
43	Canal Street	E21
23	Canberra Gardens	V11
23	Canberra Park	J3
23	Canberra Park	V11
28	Candahar Street	M13
17	Canmore Close	K11
17	Canmore Court	K11
17	Canmore Street	K11
12	Canning Place	M10
12	Canning Street	M10
17	Canning's Court	K11
18	Canterbury Street	L13
18	Canton Court	K12
29	Cappagh Gardens	N12
18	Cappy Street	N12
27	Carberry Street	K14
11	Cardigan Drive	K9
19	Carew Street	P11
17	Cargill Street	L11
7	Carlan Close	L4
19	Carlingford Street	N12
17	Carlisle Circus	L10
12	Carlisle Parade	L10
18	Carlisle Road	L10
11	Carlisle Square	L10
11	Carlisle Terrace	L10
12	Carlisle Walk	L10
17	Carlow Street	K11
7	Carmen Drive	M4
28	Carmel Street	M13
3	Carn Court	J1
3	Carn Crescent	J1
3	Carn Drive	J1
44	Carn End	S7
3	Carn Gardens	J1
3	Carn Green	J1
3	Carn Rise	J1
3	Carn Way	J1
12	Carnalea Place	M10
29	Carnamena Avenue	P14
29	Carnamena Gardens	P14
29	Carnamena Park	P14
25	Carnamona Court	G13

Page	Street	Grid Ref
17	Carnan Street	K11
24	Carnanmore Gardens	F15
24	Carnanmore Park	F15
37	Carnbrae Avenue	P16
37	Carnbrae Park	P16
30	Carncaver Road	Q14
8	Carncoole Park	K7
30	Carney Crescent	Q14
19	Carnforth Street	N11
3	Carnhill Avenue	K2
3	Carnhill Crescent	K2
3	Carnhill Drive	K2
3	Carnhill Gardens	K2
3	Carnhill Grove	K2
3	Carnhill Parade	K2
3	Carnhill Park	K2
3	Carnhill Road	K2
3	Carnmoney Road	J3
3	Carnmoney Road	K2
3	Carnmoney Road Nth	K1
16	Carnmore Place	H12
7	Carnreagh Bend	L4
3	Carntall Court	J1
3	Carntall Rise	J1
3	Carntall View	J1
3	Carntall Way	J1
42	Carntogher Road	C21
3	Carnvue Avenue	J2
3	Carnvue Court	K2
3	Carnvue Cresent	K2
3	Carnvue Drive	J2
3	Carnvue Gardens	J2
3	Carnvue Park	J2
3	Carnvue Road	J2
3	Carol Gardens	J2
3	Carol Park	J2
28	Carolan Road	M14
20	Carolhill Drive	Q10
14	Carolhill Gardens	Q10
3	Carolhill Park	H3
20	Carolhill Park	Q10
3	Carolhill Road	H3
17	Carolina Street	K11
18	Carrick Hill	L11
	(Cnoc Na Carraige)	
24	Carrigart Avenue	F14
18	Carrington Street	N12
39	Carrisbrook Gardens	D19
39	Carrisbrook Park	D19
23	Carron Walk	W12
23	Carrowreagh Gardens	W12
23	Carrowreagh Park	W12
23	Carrowreagh Road	W11
10	Carr's Glen Park	J8
38	Carson Court	B20
3	Carwood Avenue	J2
3	Carwood Crescent	J2
3	Carwood Drive	J2
3	Carwood Gardens	J2
3	Carwood Parade	J2
3	Carwood Park	J2
3	Carwood Park South	J2
3	Carwood Way	J2
30	Casaeldona Crescent	Q14
30	Casaeldona Drive	Q14
30	Casaeldona Gardens	Q14
30	Casaeldona Park	Q14
30	Casaeldona Rise	Q14
25	Casement Courts	H14
4	Cashel Close	M1
5	Cashel Drive	M1
4	Cashel Walk	M1
18	Castle Arcade	L11
42	Castle Arcade	D21
9	Castle Avenue	L7
30	Castle Court	Q14
9	Castle Drive	L7
5	Castle Gardens	L7
18	Castle Lane	L11
30	Castle Mews	Q4
8	Castle Park	K7
18	Castle Place	L11
42	Castle Street	D21
18	Castle Street	L11
35	Castleboy Avenue	M16
36	Castlecoole Lodge	M16
35	Castlecoole Park	M17

Page	Street	Grid Ref
36	Castlecoole Walk	M16
36	Castledillon Road	M17
30	Castlegrange	R14
21	Castlehill Drive	S11
30	Castlehill Farm	R14
21	Castlehill Manor	S11
21	Castlehill Park	S11
21	Castlehill Road West	S11
21	Castlehill Road	S11
35	Castlehume Gardens	M17
21	Castlekaria Manor	S11
30	Castlemore Avenue	Q14
30	Castlemore Park	Q14
21	Castleorr Manor	S11
19	Castlereagh Parade	P12
19	Castlereagh Place	N12
19	Castlereagh Road	P13
19	Castlereagh Street	N12
35	Castlerobin Lodge	M16
35	Castlerobin Road	M16
12	Castleton Avenue	M9
27	Castleton Court	K14
11	Castleton Gardens	L9
21	Castleview Cottage Gdns	S12
30	Castleview Court	R13
30	Castleview Road	S12
20	Castleview Terrace	Q11
35	Castleward Park	M16
25	Castlewood Manor	G15
18	Catherine Street	M12
18	Catherine Street North	M12
41	Causeway End Gardens	B21
41	Causeway End Park	B21
41	Causeway End Road	C21
41	Causeway Manor	B21
25	Cavanmore Gardens	G14
8	Cavehill Drive	K7
11	Cavehill Road	K8
17	Cavendish Court	J11
	(Cuirt Chaibhendis)	
17	Cavendish Square	K12
17	Cavendish Street	J12
17	Cawnpore Street	J11
27	Cawra Court	L13
11	Cedar Avenue	K9
14	Cedar Grove	R9
3	Cedar Hill	J1
36	Cedarhurst Court	N17
36	Cedarhurst Rise	M17
36	Cedarhurst Road	M17
17	Centurion Street	J11
17	*Centurion Way	K11
	(Lawnbourne Avenue)	
11	Century Street	K10
3	Ceylon Street	J11
19	Chadolly Street	N11
27	Chadwick Street	K13
19	Chamberlain Street	N11
18	Chambers Street	L12
22	Chandlers Court	U13
19	Channing Street	P12
42	Chapel Hill	D21
18	Chapel Lane	L11
17	Charles Street South	L12
27	Charleville Avenue	K14
17	Charleville Street	K10
18	Charlotte Street	M12
11	Charnwood Avenue	K8
11	Charnwood Court	K8
31	Charters Avenue	S13
37	Chartwell Park	N16
19	Chater Street	P11
39	Chatsworth Gdns	C19
19	Chatsworth Street	N12
19	Chelsea Street	P11
29	Cheltenham Gardens	N14
29	Cheltenham Park	N14
19	Chemical Street	N11
	(Sraid na gCeimicean)	
32	Cherry Close	F16
32	Cherry Court	F16
32	Cherry Drive	F16
32	Cherry Gardens	F19
39	Cherry Lane	C20
3	Cherry Meadows	J3
32	Cherry Park	F16
32	Cherry Road	F16

STREET INDEX

Page	Street	Grid Ref
20	Cherry Tree Walk	R12
32	Cherry Walk	F16
42	Cherry Vale	D22
27	Cherryhill	L14
22	Cherryhill Avenue	U11
23	Cherryhill Crescent	V11
22	Cherryhill Drive	U11
22	Cherryhill Gardens	U11
22	Cherryhill Park	U11
23	Cherryhill Road	V11
23	Cherryhill Walk	V11
4	Cherrylands	M2
3	Cherrymount	K1
21	Cherrytree	S13
3	Cherryvale Avenue	J3
3	Cherryvale Drive	J3
3	Cherryvale Park	J3
20	Cherryvalley	R12
21	Cherryvalley Gardens	S12
20	Cherryvalley Green	R12
21	Cherryvalley Park	R12
21	Cherryvalley Pk West	R13
19	Cherryville Street	N12
29	Chesham Crescent	N13
29	Chesham Drive	N13
29	Chesham Gardens	N13
29	Chesham Grove	N13
29	Chesham Parade	N13
29	Chesham Park	N13
29	Chesham Terrace	N13
28	Chesterfield Park	N14
11	Chestnut Gardens	K9
11	Chestnut Grove	L8
5	Chestnut Hill	P2
32	Chestnut Hill	E18
32	Chestnut Hollow	E18
32	Chestnut Park	F16
19	Cheviot Avenue	P11
19	Cheviot Street	P11
11	Chichester Avenue	L8
11	Chichester Close	L8
11	Chichester Court	L8
11	Chichester Gardens	L8
11	Chichester Mews	K8
11	Chichester Pk Central	K8
11	Chichester Park North	K8
11	Chichester Park South	L8
11	Chichester Road	L8
18	Chichester Street	M11
11	Chief Street	J10
34	Chippendale Court	H16
34	Chippendale Gardens	H16
27	Chlorine Gardens	L13
19	Chobham Street	P11
17	Christian Place	K11
4	Christine Drive	K1
4	Christine Gardens	K1
4	Christine Grove	K1
4	Christine Park	K1
4	Christine Road	K1
44	Church Avenue	T6
33	Church Avenue	G17
5	Church Avenue	N1
3	Church Crescent	K3
3	Church Crescent	K3
3	Church Drive	K3
32	Church Glen	E18
44	Church Green	S6
22	Church Green	U12
44	Church Hill	S6
40	Church Hill	F19
18	Church Lane	M11
43	Church Lane	F21
42	Church Lane	D21
3	Church Park	K3
3	Church Road	J3
3	Church Road	K3
7	Church Road	L4
28	Church Road	N15
30	Church Road	Q14
44	Church Road	T7
23	Church Road	V12
18	Church Street	L11
44	Church View	S7
32	Church View	F16
44	Church View Mews	S6
3	Church Way	K3
31	Church Wynd	S13
11	Churchill Street	L10
14	Churchland Close	R9
11	*Churchview Court	K10
	(Glenview Street)	
29	Cicero Gardens	P13
5	Circular Road	N2
20	Circular Road	R10
17	City Walk	L12
17	City Way	L12
23	Claggan Gardens	V12
23	*Claggan Park	V12
	(Claggan Gardens)	
23	Claggan Walk	V12
44	Clanbrassil Road	T5
11	Clanchattan Street	L9
19	Clandeboye Drive	N11
	(Ceide Chlann Aodha Bui)	
19	Clandeboye Gardens	N11
	(Gairdini Chlann Aodha Bui)	
19	Clandeboye Street	N12
12	Clanmorris Street	M10
19	Clanroy Parade	Q11
19	Clara Avenue	P12
19	Clara Cresent Lower	P12
19	Clara Cresent Upper	P12
20	Clara Park	Q12
20	Clara Road	Q12
19	Clara Street	N12
20	Clara Way	Q12
20	Clarawood Crescent	Q13
20	Clarawood Drive	Q13
20	Clarawood Grove	Q13
20	Clarawood Park	Q13
20	Clarawood Walk	Q12
10	Clare Gardens	J8
7	Clare Gardens	M4
10	Clare Glen	J8
10	Clare Glen	J8
10	Clare Heights	J8
10	Clare Hill	J8
41	Clarehill Court	B21
15	Clarehill Lane	S8
44	Clarehill Mews	S7
17	Claremont Court	L13
27	Claremont Mews	L13
44	Claremont Road	T6
17	Claremont Street	L13
18	*Clarence Place Mews	L11
	(Upper Arthur Street)	
18	Clarence Street	P12
18	Clarence Street West	L12
18	Clarendon Avenue	P12
18	Clarendon Road	M10
18	*Clarke's Lane	L11
	(Curtis Street)	
27	Cleaver Avenue	L14
27	Cleaver Court	L14
27	Cleaver Gardens	L14
27	Cleaver Park	L14
17	Clementine Drive	L12
17	Clementine Gardens	L12
17	Clementine Park	L12
36	Cleveley Park	N16
11	Clifton Crescent	K9
11	Clifton Drive	K9
18	Clifton House Mews	L10
11	Clifton Park Court	L10
11	Clifton Street	L10
11	Cliftondene Crescent	J9
11	Cliftondene Gardens	J9
11	Cliftondene Park	J9
11	Cliftonpark Avenue	K10
11	Cliftonville Avenue	L9
11	Cliftonville Drive	K9
11	Cliftonville Parade	K9
11	Cliftonville Road	K9
11	Cliftonville Street	K9
37	Cliveden Crescent	N16
21	Cloghan Cresent	T12
34	Cloghan Gardens	H16
21	Cloghan Gardens	T12
21	Cloghan Park	T12
43	Clogher Road	F22
21	Clonallon Court	Q11
20	Clonallon Gardens	Q11
20	Clonallon Park	Q11
17	Clonard Court	K11
17	Clonard Crescent	K11
	(Corran Chluain Ard)	
17	Clonard Gardens	J11
17	Clonard Heights	K11
	(Ard Chluain Ard)	
17	Clonard Place	K11
	(Plas Chluain Ard)	
17	Clonard Rise	K11
	(Mala Chluain Ard)	
17	Clonard Street	K11
5	Clonaslea	N1
20	Clonaver Cresent Nth	Q10
20	Clonaver Crescent Sth	Q10
20	Clonaver Drive	Q11
20	Clonaver Park	Q10
7	Clonbeg Drive	M4
16	Clondara Parade	J13
16	Clondara Street	J13
30	Clonduff Drive	Q4
25	Clonelly Avenue	G14
42	Clonlee Park	D21
17	Clonfaddan Crescent	L11
17	Clonfaddan Street	L11
19	Clonlee Drive	Q11
7	Clonmore Drive	L4
40	Clonmore Park	E20
7	Clonmore Walk	L4
39	Clontara Park	D19
37	Clontonacally Road	Q17
24	Cloona Avenue	F15
24	Cloona Crescent	F15
24	Cloona Park	F15
24	Cloona Park	F15
27	Cloreen Park	L13
25	Closnamona Court	G13
5	Cloughfern Avenue	M2
2	Cloughmore Road	G3
16	Clovelly Street	J11
39	Cloverdale Crescent	D19
39	Cloverdale Road	D19
43	Cloverhill Avenue	E22
21	Cloverhill Gardens	S11
21	Cloverhill Park	S10
16	Clowney Street	J11
4	Cloyne Crescent	M1
17	Cluain Mor Avenue	J12
16	Cluain Mor Close	J12
16	Cluain Mor Drive	J12
16	Cluain Mor Gardens	J12
16	Cluain Mor Lane	J12
16	Cluain Mor Park	J12
7	Cluan Place	M11
18	Clyde Court	N11
	(Cuirt Chluaidh)	
18	*Coar's Lane	L11
	(Curtis Street)	
19	Coburg Street	N12
36	Colby Park	N16
17	Colchester Park	K12
28	Colenso Court	L13
28	Colenso Parade	L13
18	Cole's Alley	M11
35	Coleshill Gardens	M16
24	Colin Grove	E15
24	Colin Road	E15
24	Colinbrook	E15
24	Colinbrook Avenue	E15
24	Colinbrook Close	E15
24	Colinbrook Crescent	E15
24	Colinbrook Drive	E15
24	Colinbrook Gardens	E15
24	Colinbrook Green	E15
24	Colinbrook Park	E15
33	Colindale Park	F16
25	Colinglen Park	E14
24	Colinglen Road	D15
24	Colinmill	E15
17	Colinpark Street	J11
	(Sraid Phairc Chollan)	
9	Colinton Gardens	L6
24	Colinvale	E14
24	Colinvale	E15
24	Colinvale	E15
32	Colinview	F18
17	Colinview Street	J11
	(Sraid Radharc Chollan)	
17	Colinward Street	J11
	(Sraid Bharda Chollan)	
24	Colinwell Road	D15
27	College Gardens	L13
17	College Avenue	L11
18	College Court	L11
18	College Green	L13
18	College Green Mews	L13
28	College Park	L13
28	College Park	L13
28	College Park Avenue	L13
28	College Park East	L13
17	College Place North	L11
17	College Square East	L11
17	College Square North	L11
18	College Street Mews	L11
18	College Street	L11
17	Colligan Street	K12
25	Collin Gardens	G14
6	Collinbridge Close	J4
6	Collinbridge Court	J4
6	Collinbridge Drive	J4
6	Collinbridge Gardens	J4
6	Collinbridge Park	J4
6	Collinbridge Road	K4
28	Collingwood Avenue	M13
28	Collingwood Road	M13
6	Collinward Avenue	K4
3	Collinward Crescent	K3
3	Collinward Drive	K3
4	Collinward Gardens	K3
3	Collinward Grove	K3
6	Collinward Park	K4
11	Columbia Street	J10
19	Colvil Street	P11
19	Comber Court	N11
19	Comber Gardens	N11
22	Comber Road	U12
17	*Combermere Street	L12
	(Stroud Street)	
25	Commedagh Drive	H14
18	Commercial Court	L11
2	Commercial Way	H3
36	Commons Brae	N16
18	Conduit Street	L12
17	Coniston Close	K10
17	Connaught Street	K12
19	Conney Warren Lane	H8
19	Connsbank Road	P10
19	Connsbrook Avenue	P11
19	Connsbrook Drive	P11
19	Connsbrook Park	P10
19	Connswater Grove	P11
19	Connswater Link	P11
19	Connswater Mews	P11
19	Connswater Street	P11
25	Conor Rise	G14
19	Constance Street	N12
19	Convention Court	N11
19	*Convention Walk	N11
	(Convention Court)	
17	Conway Court	K11
32	Conway Lane	F18
32	Conway Lane	F18
17	Conway Link	K11
42	Conway Street	D21
17	Conway Street	K11
17	Conway Street	K11
17	Conway Walk	K11
18	Cooke Court	M12
18	Cooke Mews	M12
18	Cooke Place	M12
18	Cooke Street	M12
11	Cooldarragh Park	K8
11	Cooldarragh Park Nth	K7
3	Coolderry Gardens	M4
5	Coole Park	K3
5	Cooleen Park	N2
3	Coolehill Crescent	J3
3	Coolehill Park	J3
3	Coolemoyne Park	N2
17	Coolfin Street	K13
3	Coolmore Street	K13
9	Coolmoyne Park	L7
25	Coolnasilla Avenue	G14
25	Coolnasilla Close	G14

STREET INDEX

Page		Grid Ref	Page		Grid Ref	Page		Grid Ref	Page		Grid Ref
25	Coolnasilla Drive	G14	44	Croft Rise	T6	17	Dayton Street	L11	17	Distillery Court	K12
25	Coolnasilla Gardens	G14	44	Croft Road	T6	33	De Beere Court	H16	17	Distillery Street	K12
25	Coolnasilla Park	G13	21	Crofthouse Court	T12	12	Deacon Street	L9	18	*Distillery Walk	K12
25	Coolnasilla Park East	G14	44	Crofton Glen	T6	11	Deanby Gardens	K9		(Distillery Street)	
25	Coolnasilla Park South	G14	18	Cromac Avenue	M12	19	Dee Street	N11	18	Distillery Way	K12
25	Coolnasilla Park West	G14	18	Cromac Place	M12	7	Deerfin Park	L4	18	Divis Court	L11
37	Coolpark Avenue	N16	18	Cromac Quay	M12	10	Deerpark Drive	FJ9	16	Divis Drive	H13
42	Coolsara Park	D21	18	Cromac Square	M12	10	Deerpark Gardens	J9	17	Divis Street	L11
4	Coolshannagh Park	M3	18	Cromac Street	M12	11	Deerpark Grove	K9	42	Divis Way	C21
11	Coombe Hill Park	J8	12	Cromarty Place	V12	10	Deerpark Parade	J9	16	Divismore Crescent	H12
29	Cooneen Way	N14	42	Crommelin Place	D22	10	Deerpark Road	J9	16	Divismore Park	H12
38	Corby Drive	C20	12	Cromwell Road	L12	10	Deerpark Road	J9	16	Divismore Way	H12
25	Corby Way	G14	43	Cromwell's Close	E21	20	Dehra Grove	Q11	4	Doagh Road	L1
30	Cormorant Park	R14	43	Cromwell's Highway	E21	40	Delacherois Avenue	E21	4	Doagh Road	M3
18	Corn Market	L11	17	Crosby Street	K11	30	Delamont Park	Q14	39	Dock Street	M11
5	Coronation Drive	N1	28	Cross Parade	M13	12	Delaware Street	N12	39	Dog Kennel Close	C20
22	Coronation Park	U13	42	Crossan Walk	C22	37	Delgany Avenue	P16	39	Dog Kennel Crescent	C20
18	Corporation Square	M11	39	Crossbill Place	C20	18	Delhi Parade	M13	39	Dog Kennel Lane	C20
18	Corporation Street	M11	12	Crosscollyer Street	L9	28	Delhi Street	M13	25	Doire Beg	G14
25	Corrib Avenue	F14	17	Crossland Court	K11	44	Demesne Avenue	T7	10	Donaldson Crescent	J10
32	Corrina Avenue	F16	12	Crossland Street	K11	44	Demesne Close	T7	42	Donard Drive	C21
32	Corrina Park	F16	7	Crossreagh Drive	L4	44	Demesne Grove	T7	18	Donard Street	N12
12	Corry Link	M10	18	Crown Entry	L11	44	Demesne Manor	T7	18	Donegal Arcade	L11
12	Corry Place	M10	10	Crumlin Gardens	J10	44	Demesne Park	T7	18	Donegall Avenue	K13
12	Corry Road	M10	10	Crumlin Road	H8	44	Demesne Road	T7	17	Donegall Gardens	K13
12	Cosgrave Court	L10	10	Crumlin Road	H9	44	Demesne Road	T7	18	Donegall Lane	L11
12	Cosgrave Heights	L10	11	Crumlin Road	J10	41	Demiville Avenue	A22	25	Donegall Park	H13
12	Cosgrave Street	L10	19	Crystal Street	P12	25	Denewood Drive	H13	9	Donegall Park Avenue	L7
33	Cotlands Green	F16	19	Cuan Parade	J11	25	Denewood Park	H13	18	Donegall Pass	L12
37	Cotswold Avenue	N16	17	Cullingtree Road	K12	17	Denmark Street	L10	18	Donegall Parade	K13
38	Cottage Gardens	B19	12	Culmeglen	N2	20	Dennet End	N14	18	Donegall Place	L11
42	Coulson Avenue	D22	25	Culmore Gardens	F14	20	Denorrton Park	Q10	18	Donegall Quay	M11
17	Courtrai Street	K10	23	Culross Drive	W12	28	Depot Road	Q9	18	Donegall Road	J12
12	Coyle Street	M12	23	Culross Place	W12	28	Deramore Avenue	M14	18	Donegall Road	L12
42	Craig Crescent	C22	18	Cultra Street	M10	28	Deramore Drive	K15	18	Donegall Square East	L11
42	Craig Gardens	C22	22	Cumberland Avenue	U12	28	Deramore Gardens	M14	18	Donegall Square Mews	L12
3	Craiglands Drive	J1	22	Cumberland Close	U12	27	Deramore Park	K15	18	Donegall Square North	L11
3	Craiglands Manor	J1	22	Cumberland Court	U12	27	Deramore Park South	K15	18	Donegall Square South	L12
23	Craigleith Drive	V12	22	Cumberland Drive	U12	28	Deramore Street	M14	18	Donegall Square West	L11
23	Craigleith Walk	V12	22	Cumberland Lane	U12	28	Derlett Street	M13	18	Donegall Street Place	L11
42	Craigmore Road	C21	22	Cumberland Mews	U12	16	Dermott Hill Drive	G12	18	Donegall Street	L11
18	Craigmore Way	L12	22	Cumberland Park	U12	16	Dermott Hill Gardens	G12	25	Donegore Gardens	F15
23	Craignish Court	V12	22	Cumberland Road	U12	16	Dermott Hill Grove	G12	27	Donnybrook Street	K13
23	Craignish Crescent	V11	17	*Cumberland Street	K11	16	Dermott Hill Grove	G12	10	Donore Court	L10
44	Craigtara	S7		(Carlow Street)		16	Dermott Hill Parade	G12	29	Donovan Parade	P13
10	Cranbrook Court	J9	22	Cumberland Walk	K11	16	Dermott Hill Park	G12	25	Doon Cottages	F15
12	Cranbrook Gardens	J9	19	Cuming Road	N11	16	Dermott Hill Road	G12	34	Doon End	H16
11	Cranburn Street	L10	42	Cumnor Walk	W12	16	Dermott Hill Way	G12	25	Doon Road	F15
34	Cranfield Gardens	H16	17	Cupar Street	J11	32	Derriaghy Road	D18	4	Doonbeg Drive	L3
27	Cranmore Avenue	K14	11	Cupar Way	K11	39	Derriaghy Road	C19	3	Dorchester Avenue	H2
27	Cranmore Gardens	K14	18	Curtis Street	L11	25	Derrin Pass	H14	3	Dorchester Crescent	H2
27	Cranmore Park	K14	42	Curtis Walk	D22	42	Derrin Place	C21	3	Dorchester Drive	H2
17	Craven Street	K11	28	Curzon Street	M13	7	Derry Hill	L4	3	Dorchester Gardens	H2
30	Crawford Park	Q14	18	Cussick Street	K13	12	Derry Road	J3	3	Dorchester Park	H2
32	Credenhill Park	F16	18	Custom House Square	M11	4	Derrycoole Park	M3	39	Dorchester Park	C19
32	Credenhill Park	F16	33	Cypress Close	G18	4	Derrycoole Way	L4	27	Dorchester Park	K16
24	Creeslough Court	F14	20	Cyprus Avenue	Q12	4	Derrycoole Walk	M3	23	Dornock Place	V12
24	Creeslough Gardens	F14	20	Cyprus Gardens	Q12	27	Derrymore Avenue	J3	20	Douglas Court	Q11
24	Creeslough Park	F14	20	Cyprus Park	Q12	27	Derryvolgie Avenue	K13	17	Dover Place	K11
24	Creeslough Walk	F14				27	Derryvolgie Mews	K13	17	Dover Court	L11
42	Creeve Place	C21		**DAIRY STREET**	**J12**	40	Derryvolgie Park	E19	2	Dover Road	G3
16	Creeve Walk	H14	25	Creeve Walk	H14	11	Derwent Street	N11	17	Dover Street	L11
30	Creevy Avenue	R13	17	Daisyfield Street	K10	5	Devenish Court	K11	17	Dover Walk	L11
30	Creevy Way	R13	39	Dalboyne Court	E20	5	Devenish Drive	M1	16	Downfine Gardens	G13
29	Cregagh Court	P13	39	Dalboyne Gardens	D20	5	Devenish Walk	N1	16	Downfine Park	H13
29	Cregagh Park	P14	39	Dalboyne Park	D20	19	Devon Drive	P11	16	Downfine Walk	H13
29	Cregagh Park East	P14	25	Dalebrook Avenue	G15	20	Devon Parade	P11	4	Downhill Avenue	L1
29	Cregagh Road	P13	25	Dalebrook Park	G15	17	Devonshire Close	K12	35	Downhill Avenue	L17
19	Cregagh Street	N13	3	Dalewood	H2	17	Devonshire Place	K12	4	Downhill Park	L1
32	Creighton Manor	E17	23	Dalkeith Gardens	V12	17	Devonshire Street	K12	35	Downhill Walk	L17
32	Creighton Mews	E17	5	Dalriada Avenue	P2	17	Devonshire Way	K12	35	Downhill Walk	L17
32	Creighton Road	F16	5	Dalriada Drive	P2	17	Dewey Street	K10	17	Downing Street	K11
18	Crescent Gardens	L13	5	Dalriada Avenue	P2	5	Dhu-Varren Crescent	J11	5	Downpatrick Green	M1
35	Crevenish Walk	M16	21	Dalry Park	T12	11	Dhu-Varren Parade	J11	19	Downpatrick Street	P11
28	Cricklewood Crescent	L15	18	Dalton Street	M11	5	Dhu-Varren Park	J11	44	Downshire Mews	S7
28	Cricklewood Park	L15	28	Damascus Street	M13	25	Diamond Avenue	H15	29	Downshire Parade	P14
17	Crimea Close	K10	27	Danesfort	K14	25	Diamond Gardens	H15	29	Downshire Park East	P14
17	Crimea Court	K11	11	Dann's Row	M12	26	Diamond Gardens	H15	29	Downshire Park Central	P14
17	Crimea Street	K10	17	Danube Street	K10	25	Diamond Grove	H15	29	Downshire Park North	P14
32	Croaghan Gardens	G14	11	Daphne Street	K12	43	Dill Avenue	E22	44	Downshire Park South	P14
17	Crocus Street	K12	12	Dargan Crescent	N8	29	Dill Road	P13	18	Downshire Place	L12
37	Croft Cottages	P17	13	Dargan Drive	N8	5	Dillon's Avenue	N3	44	Downshire Place	S7
44	Croft Gardens	T6	13	Dargan Road	N8	5	Dillon's Court	N3	44	Downshire Road	S7
44	Croft Hill	P17	4	Dart Hill	H4	17	Disraeli Close	J10	29	Downshire Road	P14
44	Croft Manor	T6	23	Davarr Avenue	V12	17	Disraeli Court	J10	9	Downview Avenue	L7
44	Croft Meadows	T6	17	David Street	K11	11	Disraeli Street	J10	9	Downview Drive	L7
44	Croft Park	T6	11	Dawson Street	L10	11	Disraeli Walk	J10	9	Downview Gardens	L7

50

STREET INDEX

Page	Street	Grid Ref
9	Downview Lodge	L6
9	Downview Mews	L7
9	Downview Park	L7
8	Downview Park West	K7
25	Drenia	G15
42	Dromara Park	C22
28	Dromara Street	M13
3	Dromore Street	N13
23	Drumadoon Drive	V12
23	Drumadoon Drive	V12
23	Drumadoon Park	V12
41	Drumard Court	B21
41	Drumard Crescent	C21
41	Drumard Drive	B21
41	Drumard Grange	B21
38	Drumard Park	B21
35	Drumart Drive	M17
35	Drumart Gardens	M17
35	Drumart Green	M17
35	Drumart Square	M17
35	Drumart Walk	L17
42	Drumbeg Court	C22
42	Drumbeg Drive	C22
35	Drumcairn Close	L17
7	Drumcor Green	L4
7	Drumcree Place	L4
29	Drumkeen Court	N15
28	Drumkeen Manor	N15
41	Drumlough Gardens	B22
27	Drummond Park	J16
29	Drumragh End	N14
34	Dub Lane	J16
34	Dub Mews	J16
18	Dublin Road	L12
18	Dublin Street	N12
18	Dudley Street	M13
5	Dufferin Road	H10
16	Duffield Park	H10
19	Duke Street	N11
4	Dunanney	L3
18	Dunbar Link	M11
18	Dunbar Street	M11
11	Dunblane Avenue	FJ9
6	Dunboyne Park	H11
11	Duncairn Avenue	L10
12	Duncairn Gardens	L10
12	Duncairn Parade	L10
39	Duncan's Road	C20
8	Duncoole Park	K7
12	Duncrue Crescent	M8
12	Duncrue Link	M8
12	Duncrue Pass	M8
12	Duncrue Place	M8
12	Duncrue Road	M8
12	Duncrue Street	M9
12	Duncrue Street	M10
17	Dundee Street	K11
19	Dundela Avenue	Q11
19	Dundela Close	Q11
19	Dundela Court	Q11
19	Dundela Cresent	Q11
19	Dundela Drive	Q11
19	Dundela Flats	Q11
20	Dundela Gardens	Q11
19	Dundela Park	P11
19	Dundela Street	Q11
19	Dundela View	Q11
22	Dundonald Heights	U12
42	Dundrod Court	C22
42	Dundrod Drive	C22
42	Dundrod Walk	C22
11	Duneden Park	J9
24	Dungloe Crescent	F14
23	Dungoyne Park	V12
11	Dunkeld Gardens	J9
23	Dunlady Manor	V11
23	Dunlady Manor	V11
23	Dunlady Road	V11
12	Dunlambert Avenue	L8
12	Dunlambert Drive	L8
12	Dunlambert Gardens	L8
12	Dunlambert Park	L8
12	Dunleady Park	V11
12	Dunlewey Street	K11
17	Dunlewey Walk	K11
7	Dunloy Gardens	L4
17	Dunluce Avenue	K13
25	Dunmisk Park	H14
11	Dunmore Street	L9
11	Dunmore Drive	L9
17	Dunmore Park	K11
17	Dunmoyle Street	J11
33	Dunmurry Lane	G12
25	Dunmurry Lodge	G16
23	Dunoon Park	V12
11	Dunowen Gardens	K9
4	Dunowen Pass	L3
19	Dunraven Avenue	P12
19	Dunraven Court	P12
19	Dunraven Crescent	P12
19	Dunraven Drive	P12
19	Dunraven Gardens	P12
19	Dunraven Parade	P12
19	Dunraven Park	P12
19	Dunraven Park	P12
35	Dunseverick Avenue	M17
5	Dunsona Avenue	P2
5	Dunsona Drive	P2
5	Dunsona Park	P2
23	Dunure Park	V12
18	Dunvegan Street	N12
17	Dunville Street	K12
17	Durham Court	L11
17	Durham Street	L11
23	Durness Walk	V12
43	EAGLE TERRACE	E21
44	Ean Hill	S7
12	Earl Close	L10
29	Earl Haig Crescent	N13
29	Earl Haig Gardens	N13
29	Earl Haig Park	N13
17	Earlscourt Street	J12
20	Earlswood Grove	Q11
20	Earlswood Park	Q11
20	Earlswood Road	Q11
19	East Bread Street	P11
18	East Bridge Street	M12
43	East Down View	E21
44	East Link	S7
22	East Link Road	U12
13	East Twin Road	P9
7	East Way	M4
20	Eastleigh Cresent	Q12
20	Eastleigh Dale	R11
20	Eastleigh Drive	Q11
11	Easton Avenue	K9
11	Easton Crescent	K9
18	Eblana Street	L13
17	Ebor Drive	K13
17	Ebor Parade	K13
17	Ebor Street	K13
17	Ebor Street	K13
19	Ebrington Gardens	Q11
11	Eccles Street	K10
11	Edenbrook Close	K10
34	Edenderry Cottages	K18
34	Edenderry Road	J17
11	Edenderry Street	K10
25	Edenmore Drive	G14
20	Edenvale Court	Q11
38	Edenvale Court	B20
20	Edenvale Cresent	Q11
20	Edenvale Drive	Q11
38	Edenvale Gardens	B20
20	Edenvale Gardens	Q11
20	Edenvale Grove	Q11
33	Edenvale Meadows	G16
33	Edenvale Park	G16
20	Edenvale Park	Q11
19	Edgar Street	N11
20	Edgecumbe Drive	Q11
20	Edgecumbe Gardens	Q11
20	Edgecumbe Park	Q11
20	Edgecumbe View	Q11
42	Edgehill Park	D22
43	Edgewater	E22
13	Edgewater Road	N8
44	Edinburgh Court	T7
27	Edinburgh Mews	K13
27	Edinburgh Street	K13
27	Edith Street	N12
12	Edlingham Street	L10
18	Edward Street	L11
17	Edwina Street	K11
17	Egeria Street	K12
27	Eglantine Avenue	L13
27	Eglantine Gardens	L13
27	Eglantine Place	L13
17	Egmont Gardens	L12
11	Eia Street	L9
27	Eileen Gardens	K12
28	Elaine Street	L13
3	Elderburn	K1
29	Elesington Court	P13
28	Elgin Court	M13
28	Elgin Street	M13
11	Elimgrove Street	K10
18	Eliza Street	M12
18	Eliza Street Terrace	M12
18	Eliza Street Close	M12
44	Elizabeth Road	T7
33	Elm Corner	F17
3	Elm Court	J3
18	Elm Street	L12
19	Elmdale Street	P12
6	Elmfield Avenue	K4
6	Elmfield Crescent	K4
6	Elmfield Drive	K4
6	Elmfield Park	K4
3	Elmfield Road	K3
11	Elmfield Street	J10
19	Elmgrove Manor	P12
19	Elmgrove Road	P12
17	Elmwood Avenue	L13
42	Elmwood Drive	D22
3	Elmwood Grove	H1
17	Elmwood Mews	L13
39	Elmwood Park	E20
31	Elsmere Heights	T13
31	Elsmere Manor	T13
31	Elsmere Park	T13
17	Elswick Street	J11
	(Sraid Elswick)	
19	Emerald Street	N12
17	Empire Drive	K12
17	Empire Parade	K12
17	Empire Street	K12
11	Enfield Drive	J10
11	Enfield Parade	J10
17	Enfield Street	J10
20	Enid Drive	Q12
20	Enid Parade	Q12
23	Enler Close	V12
23	Enler East Walk	V12
23	Enler Park	V12
23	Enler Park Central	V12
23	Enler Park East	V12
23	Enler Park West	V12
4	Enniskeen Avenue	L3
41	Enterprise Crescent	B21
19	Epworth Street	N12
18	Erin Way	L12
33	Erinvale Avenue	H16
33	Erinvale Drive	H16
33	Erinvale Gardens	H16
33	Erinvale Park	H16
25	Errigal Park	G14
25	Erris Grove	F15
19	Erskine Street	N11
11	Eskdale Gardens	J9
39	Esker Ridge	C20
30	Espie Way	Q13
18	Essex Street	M13
12	Esther Street	L9
10	Estoril Court	J9
11	Estoril Park	J9
27	Ethel Street	K13
11	Etna Drive	J9
17	Eureka Drive	L12
19	Euston Street	N12
17	Euterpe Street	K12
19	Evelyn Avenue	P11
19	Evelyn Gardens	K8
19	Eversleigh Street	N12
29	Everton Drive	P14
11	Evewilliam Park	L8
11	Evolina Street	L10
18	Exchange Place	L11
18	*Exchange Street	L11
	(Edward Street)	
18	Exchange Street West	L11
17	Excise Walk	K12
10	FABURN PARK	H9
19	Factory Street	P12
40	Fairfield	E20
38	Fairhaven Park	B20
11	Fairfax Court	K10
3	Fairhill Crescent	K2
3	Fairhill Drive	K2
3	Fairhill Gardens	K2
9	Fairhill Gardens	L7
3	Fairhill Green	K2
3	Fairhill Park	K2
9	Fairhill Park	L7
3	Fairhill Road	K2
9	Fairhill Walk	L7
9	Fairhill Way	L7
40	Fairtree Hill	E19
4	Fairview Avenue	K1
4	Fairview Cresent	K1
4	Fairview Drive	K1
3	Fairview Gardens	K1
4	Fairview Grove	K1
4	Fairview Parade	K1
4	Fairview Park	K1
32	Fairview Park	E18
4	Fairview Road	K1
17	Fairview Street	L10
4	Fairview Way	K1
34	Fairway Avenue	J16
34	Fairway Crescent	J16
34	Fairway Drive	J16
34	Fairway Gardens	J16
30	Fairway Gardens	R13
6	Fairyknowe Drive	K4
6	Fairyknowe Gardens	L4
6	Fairyknowe Park	L4
24	Falcarragh Drive	F14
27	Falcon Road	K14
17	Falls Court	K11
	(Cuirt na bhFal)	
17	Falls Road	J12
	(Bothar na bhFal)	
17	Fallswater Drive	J12
17	Fallswater Street	J12
17	Fane Street	K13
44	Farmhill Lane	T5
44	Farmhill Road	T6
31	Farmhurst Green	S13
31	Farmhurst Way	S13
3	Farmley Cresent	J3
3	Farmley Gardens	J3
6	Farmley Mews	J4
3	Farmley Park	J3
3	Farmley Road	J3
18	Farnham Street	M13
3	Farrier Court	J3
10	Farringdon Court	J9
11	Farringdon Gardens	J9
19	Fashoda Street	P12
13	Federation Street	N13
17	Felt Street	L12
20	Ferguson Drive	Q11
41	Ferguson Drive	A21
41	Ferguson Road	A21
19	Fern Street	N11
5	Fernagh Avenue	N3
5	Fernagh Court	N3
5	Fernagh Drive	N3
5	Fernagh Gardens	N3
5	Fernagh Parade	N3
5	Fernagh Road	M3
39	Fernbank	D20
43	Ferndale Avenue	E22
3	Ferndale Avenue	K2
27	Ferndale Court	K14
3	Ferndale Crescent	J2
3	Ferndale Drive	J2
3	Ferndale Gardens	J2
3	Ferndale Grove	J2
3	Ferndale Parade	K2
3	Ferndale Park	J2
3	Ferndale Road	J2
27	Ferndale Street	K14
27	Ferndale Place	K14
39	Ferndell	E20

STREET INDEX

Page	Street	Grid Ref
23	Ferndene Avenue	V13
23	Ferndene Gardens	V13
23	Ferndene Park	V13
23	Ferndene Road	V13
10	Fernhill Crescent	H9
10	Fernhill Grove	H9
10	Fernhill Heights	H10
4	Fernlea Lane	L2
4	Fernlea Park	M2
19	Fernvale Street	Q10
28	Fernwood Street	M14
12	Fife Street	M9
17	Fifth Street	K11
11	*Filor Court	K10
	(Manor Drive)	
25	Finaghy Park North	H15
25	Finaghy Park Central	H16
25	Finaghy Park South	H15
25	Finaghy Road North	H15
34	Finaghy Road South	H16
34	Finbank Court	J16
34	Finbank Gardens	J16
34	Finch Close	J16
34	Finch Court	J16
39	Finch Gardens	C20
34	Finch Grove	J16
34	Finch Place	J16
34	Finch Way	J16
14	Finchley Gardens	R10
14	Finchley Park	R10
14	Finchley Vale	R10
34	Findon Gardens	J16
34	Findon Grove	J16
34	Findon Place	J16
4	Fineview	M2
11	Fingal Street	J10
17	Fingals Court	L11
7	Finlay Park	M6
19	Finmore Court	N11
11	Finn Square	L11
5	Finner Walk	M1
34	Finnis Close	J16
34	Finnis Drive	J16
34	Finnis Drive	J16
37	Finsbury Avenue	P17
37	Finsbury Crescent	P17
37	Finsbury Drive	P17
37	Finsbury Gardens	P17
37	Finsbury Park	N17
29	Finsbury Street	N13
19	Finvoy Street	P11
34	Finwood Court	J16
34	Finwood Park	J16
11	Firmount	L8
15	Firmount Crescent	S8
11	First Street	K11
17	*Fisherwick Place	L11
	(College Square East)	
18	Fitzroy Avenue	L13
18	Fitzroy Court	L13
28	Fitzwilliam Avenue	M14
28	Fitzwiiliam Square	M13
17	Fitzwilliam Street	L13
11	Flax Street	K10
10	Flaxton Place	H8
4	Fleetwood Street	L10
19	Flora St Walkway	P12
19	Flora Street	P12
6	Floral Gardens	K4
6	Floral Park	K4
6	Floral Road	K4
17	Florence Court	L10
17	Florence Place	L10
17	Florence Square	L10
17	Florence Walk	L10
28	Florenceville Ave	M14
28	Florenceville Dr	M14
19	Florida Drive	N12
18	Florida Street	N12
29	Flush Drive	N14
29	Flush Gardens	N14
29	Flush Green	N14
41	Flush Park	B22
29	Flush Park	N14
25	Fodnamona Ct	G13
40	Fontaine Place	E20
36	Forest Grove	M17
27	Forest Hill	K15
32	Forest Park	F16
17	Forest Street	J11
28	Foresthill View	N15
17	Forfar Street	J11
17	Forfar Street	J11
	(Sraid Fothar Faire)	
10	Formby Park	J8
17	Forster Street	K10
42	Fort Hill	D21
22	Fort Hill	U12
22	Fort Hill Close	U12
22	Fort Road	U13
17	Fort Street	J11
18	Forth Parade	J11
16	Forthbrook Court	H10
4	Forthill Drive	L1
4	Forthill Gardens	L2
4	Forthill Grove	L1
4	Forthill Park	L1
10	Forthriver Close	H9
10	Forthriver Cres	H9
10	Forthriver Dale	H9
10	Forthriver Drive	H9
10	Forthriver Green	H9
10	Forthriver Link	H9
10	Forthriver Parade	H9
10	Forthriver Park	H9
10	Forthriver Pass	H10
10	Forthriver Road	H9
10	Forthriver Way	H10
17	Fortuna Street	K13
12	Fortwilliam Cres	M8
9	Fortwilliam Drive	L7
12	Fortwilliam Gdns	L8
12	Fortwilliam Grange	M8
12	Fortwilliam Park	L8
12	Fortwilliam Parade	L8
18	Fountain Lane	L11
18	Fountain Street	L11
17	Fountainville Ave	L13
37	Fourwinds Ave	P16
37	Fourwinds Drive	P16
37	Fourwinds Park	P16
19	Foxglove Street	P12
17	Foyle Court	K10
4	Foyle Hill	M3
18	Francis Street	L11
19	Frank Place	N12
19	Frank Street	N12
18	Franklin St Place	L12
18	Franklin Street	L12
19	Fraser Pass	N11
19	Fraser Street	N11
18	Frederick Street	L10
17	Frenchpark Street	K13
18	Friendly Place	M12
18	Friendly Row	M12
18	Friendly Street	M12
18	Friendly Way	M12
19	Frome Street	N11
25	Fruithill Park	H14
38	Fulmar Avenue	B20
38	Fulmar Crescent	B20
18	Fulton Street	L12
17	**GAFFIKIN STREET**	L12
12	Gainsborough Dr	L9
28	Galwally Avenue	M15
28	Galwally Park	N15
22	Galway Court	U12
22	Galway Drive	U12
22	Galway Manor	U12
22	Galway Mews	U12
22	Galway Park	U12
17	Galway Street	L11
18	Gamble Street	M11
32	Garden Row	E17
32	Gardenmore Road	E17
17	Gardiner Place	L11
17	Gardiner Street	L11
37	Garland Avenue	P16
29	Garland Crescent	P15
37	Garland Green	P16
37	Garland Hill	P16
29	Garland Park	P15
12	Garmoyle Street	M10
14	Garnerville Drive	R9
14	Garnerville Gdns	R9
14	Garnerville Grove	R9
14	Garnerville Park	R9
14	Garnerville Road	R9
25	Garnock	G15
25	Garnock Hill	G15
25	Garnock Hill Park	G16
20	Garranard Manor	R10
20	Garranard Park	R10
34	Garron Crescent	H16
7	Garton Way	L5
25	Gartree Place	G14
40	Garvey Court	E20
24	Garvey Glen	F14
24	Garvey Manor	E14
40	Garvey Manor	E20
43	Garvey Terrace	E21
19	Gawn Street	P11
21	Geary Road	S13
34	Geeragh Place	H16
28	Geneva Gardens	L14
17	Genoa Street	K12
11	Geoffrey Street	K10
11	Ghent Place	K10
35	Giant's Ring Road	K17
29	Gibson Park Ave	N13
29	Gibson Park Drive	N13
29	Gibson Park Gdns	N13
17	Gibson Street	K12
31	Gilbourne Court	S13
31	Gilnahirk Avenue	S13
31	Gilnahirk Crescent	S13
31	Gilnahirk Drive	S13
31	Gilnahirk Park	S13
31	Gilnahirk Rise	S13
31	Gilnahirk Road	T13
31	Gilnahirk Rd West	T14
31	Gilnahirk Walk	S13
28	Gipsy Street	M14
11	Glandore Avenue	L8
11	Glandore Drive	L8
11	Glandore Gardens	L8
12	Glandore Parade	L9
11	Glanleam Drive	L8
4	Glanroy Crescent	M3
4	Glanroy Terrace	M3
11	Glantane Drive	L8
11	Glantrasna Drive	L8
11	Glanworth Drive	L8
11	Glanworth Gdns	L9
12	Glasgow Street	M9
25	Glassmullin Gdns	G14
9	Glastonbury Ave	L7
32	Glasvey Close	E16
32	Glasvey Court	E16
32	Glasvey Crescent	F16
32	Glasvey Drive	F16
32	Glasvey Gardens	E16
32	Glasvey Park	E16
32	Glasvey Rise	F16
32	Glasvey Walk	E16
42	Glebe Court	C22
3	Glebe Gardens	K3
3	Glebe Lodge	K2
3	Glebe Manor	K3
33	Glebe Road	G17
4	Glebe Road	K3
3	Glebe Road	J2
3	Glebe Road	J2
33	Glebe Road	G17
4	Glebe Road East	K3
3	Glebe Road West	K3
3	Glebe Villas	K3
42	Glebe Walk	C22
3	Glebecoole Ave	K3
3	Glebecoole Drive	K3
3	Glebecoole Park	K3
44	Glen Brae	T7
25	Glen Crescent	H13
5	Glen Crescent	N2
15	Glen Ebor Heights	S9
14	Glen Ebor Park	R9
25	Glen Manor	H13
25	Glen Parade	H13
30	Glen Rise	R13
15	Glen Road	S10
30	Glen Road	R14
24	Glen Road	F14
5	Glen Road	N2
25	Glen Road	H15
25	Glen Road Hts	F13
29	Glen Side	P14
33	Glenaan Avenue	G17
5	Glenabbey Ave	N2
5	Glenabbey Cres	N2
5	Glenabbey Drive	N2
16	Glenalina Cres	H12
16	Glenalina Gardens	H12
16	Glenalina Green	H12
16	Glenalina Pass	H12
16	Glenalina Park	H12
16	Glenalina Road	H12
16	Glenalina Road	H12
19	Glenallen Street	N11
17	Glenalpin Street	L12
11	Glenard Brook	K9
33	Glenariff Drive	G17
5	Glenariff Park	N2
34	Glenarm Square	J12
5	Glenavie Park	N2
5	Glenavon Park	N2
42	Glenavy Gardens	C22
38	Glenavy Road	A19
4	Glenbane Avenue	M3
32	Glenbank Close	E16
32	Glenbank Court	E16
32	Glenbank Drive	E16
10	Glenbank Parade	H9
32	Glenbank Place	H9
32	Glenbawn Avenue	E16
32	Glenbawn Close	E16
32	Glenbawn Court	E16
32	Glenbawn Cres	E16
32	Glenbawn Drive	E16
32	Glenbawn Link	E16
32	Glenbawn Park	E16
32	Glenbawn Place	E16
32	Glenbawn Square	E16
32	Glenbawn Walk	E16
37	Glenbeigh Drive	N16
3	Glenbourne Ave	J3
38	Glenbrae	B20
19	Glenbrook Ave	P12
5	Glenbroome Park	P2
10	Glenbryn Drive	J9
10	Glenbryn Gardens	J9
10	Glenbryn Parade	J9
11	Glenbryn Park	J9
17	*Glenburn Alley	L12
	(Schomberg Street)	
33	Glenburn Court	G17
33	Glenburn Ford	G17
33	Glenburn Mews	G17
11	Glenburn Park	K8
33	Glenburn Road	G17
33	Glenburn Road	G17
33	Glenburn Rd Sth	G17
10	Glencairn Cres	J10
3	Glencairn Drive	J3
3	Glencairn Park	J3
10	Glencairn Pass	H9
10	Glencairn Road	G9
10	Glencairn Street	J10
10	Glencairn Walk	H9
10	Glencairn Way	H9
9	Glencoe Park	L6
24	Glencolin Avenue	F14
24	Glencolin Close	F14
24	Glencolin Court	F14
24	Glencolin Drive	F14
24	Glencolin Grove	F14
24	Glencolin Heights	F14
24	Glencolin Manor	F14
24	Glencolin Park	F14
24	Glencolin Rise	F14
24	Glencolin Walk	F14
24	Glencolin Way	F14
12	Glencollyer St	L9
7	Glencoole House	M4
3	Glencoole Park	J3
25	Glencourt	H13

STREET INDEX

Page		Grid Ref
3	Glencraig Close	J2
3	Glencraig Gardens	J2
3	Glencraig Heights	J2
3	Glencraig Road	J2
5	Glencree Park	N2
29	Glencregagh Ct	N15
29	Glencregagh Dr	N15
29	Glencregagh Park	N15
29	Glencregagh Road	P15
3	Glencroft Gardens	J2
3	Glencroft Road	J2
33	Glendale	G16
36	Glendale Ave East	N16
36	Glendale Ave Nth	N16
36	Glendale Ave Sth	N16
36	Glendale Ave West	N16
36	Glendale Park	N16
14	Glendarragh	R9
14	Glendarragh Mews	R9
3	Glendermere Hts	K2
14	Glendhu Green	R9
14	Glendhu Manor	R9
14	Glendhu Park	R9
32	Glendowen Ave	D16
32	Glendowen Close	D16
32	Glendowen Grove	D16
32	Glendowen Park	D16
29	Glendower Street	N13
5	Glendun Court	KN2
33	Glendun Park	G17
23	Gleneagles Gdns	V12
23	Gleneagles Walk	V12
5	Gleneden Park	P2
6	Glenelm Park	K4
17	Glenfarne Street	K10
32	Glenfearna Ave	E16
32	Glenfearna Gdns	E16
32	Glenfearna Park	E16
32	Glenfearna Wood	E16
17	Glengall Lane	L12
17	Glengall Mews	L12
17	Glengall Street	L12
5	Glengarry Park	N2
24	Glengoland Ave	F15
24	Glengoland Cres	F15
24	Glengoland Gdns	F15
24	Glengoland Pde	F15
24	Glengoland Park	F15
24	Glengoland Park	F15
6	Glengormley Park	K4
33	Glenhead Avenue	G17
11	Glenhill Court	K10
25	Glenhill Park	H13
37	Glenholm Avenue	N16
37	Glenholm Cres	N16
36	Glenholm Drive	N16
37	Glenholm Park	N16
19	Glenhoy Drive	P12
19	Glenhoy Mews	P12
36	Glenhugh Cres	N17
36	Glenhugh Park	N17
9	Glenhurst Drive	L6
9	Glenhurst Gdns	L6
9	Glenhurst Parade	L6
32	Glenkeen	E16
5	Glenkeen Avenue	N1
5	Glenkeen Court	N1
5	Glenkeen Park	N1
3	Glenkyle Avenue	K1
4	Glenkyle Crescent	K1
3	Glenkyle Drive	K1
3	Glenkyle Gardens	K1
3	Glenkyle Green	K1
3	Glenkyle Park	K1
3	Glenkyle Park Ave	K1
4	Glenkyle Parade	K1
14	Glenlea Grove	R9
14	Glenlea Park	R9
23	Glenloch Gardens	R9
14	Glenluce Drive	R9
14	Glenluce Green	R9
14	Glenluce Walk	R9
15	Glenmachan Ave	S10
15	Glenmachan Drive	S10
15	Glenmachan Gro	R10
15	Glenmachan Mews	R10
15	Glenmachan Park	S9

Page		Grid Ref
17	Glenmachan Place	J13
15	Glenmachan Road	S10
15	Glenmachan Road	S9
17	Glenmachan St	K13
14	Glenmillan Drive	R10
14	Glenmillan Park	R10
40	Glenmore Court	E20
40	Glenmore Drive	E20
40	Glenmore Manor	E19
40	Glenmore Park	E20
40	Glenmore Park	E19
19	Glenmore Street	N11
40	Glenmore Tce Cottages	E20
40	Glenmore Walk	E20
7	Glenmount Road	M5
25	Glenmurry Court	H13
11	Glenpark Court	K10
11	Glenpark Street	K10
18	Glenravel Street	L10
12	Glenrosa Link	L10
12	Glenrosa Street	L10
3	Glenross Park	J2
25	Glenshane Gdns	G14
5	Glenshane Park	P2
29	Glensharragh Ave	P14
29	Glensharragh Gds	P14
29	Glensharragh Park	P14
33	Glenshesk Park	G17
10	Glenside Drive	H9
10	Glenside Park	H9
10	Glenside Parade	H9
24	Glenside Road	D14
24	Glenties Drive	F14
11	Glentilt Street	K10
18	Glentoran Place	N12
5	Glentoye Park	N2
17	Glenvale Street	J10
19	Glenvarlock St	P12
3	Glenvarna Court	J2
3	Glenvarna Drive	J2
3	Glenvarna Drive	J2
3	Glenvarna Green	J2
5	Glenvarna Manor	N2
3	Glenvarna Square	J2
3	Glenvarna Walk	J2
24	Glenveagh Drive	F14
24	Glenveagh Park	E14
30	Glenview Avenue	R14
44	Glenview Avenue	T7
5	Glenview Close	N3
11	Glenview Court	K10
5	Glenview Cres	N3
30	Glenview Cres	R14
30	Glenview Drive	R14
5	Glenview Drive	N3
30	Glenview Gardens	R14
5	Glenview Gardens	N3
30	Glenview Heights	R14
5	Glenview Park	N3
30	Glenview Park	Q14
44	Glenview Road	T7
11	Glenview Street	K10
24	Glenview Terrace	F15
5	Glenview Way	N3
5	Glenville Court	N2
5	Glenville Drive	N3
5	Glenville Green	N3
5	Glenville Manor	M2
5	Glenville Park	N2
5	Glenville Parade	N3
5	Glenville Road	N3
5	Glenville Road	N2
5	Glenville Way	N3
6	Glenwell Avenue	J4
6	Glenwell Crescent	J4
6	Glenwell Drive	J4
6	Glenwell Gardens	J4
6	Glenwell Grove	J4
6	Glenwell Park	J4
6	Glenwell Road	J4
18	Glenwherry Place	N12
5	Glenwhirry Court	N2
32	Glenwood Close	E16
32	Glenwood Copse	F18
32	Glenwood Court	E16
38	Glenwood Court	B19
32	Glenwood Cres	E16

Page		Grid Ref
24	Glenwood Drive	E16
32	Glenwood Gdns	E16
32	Glenwood Green	E16
32	Glenwood Mews	F18
32	Glenwood Park	F18
17	Glenwood Place	K11
32	Glenwood Row	F18
17	Glenwood Street	K11
32	Glenwood View	E16
32	Glenwood Walk	E16
18	Gloucester Street	M11
4	Glynn Park	L3
24	Good Shepherd Road	E15
18	Gordon Street	M11
17	Gortfin Street	J12
31	Gortgrib Drive	S13
21	Gortin Drive	S12
21	Gortin Park	S12
31	Gortland Avenue	S13
31	Gortland Park	S13
31	Gortlands Mews	S13
42	Gortmore Park	C21
4	Gortmore Terrace	M3
25	Gortnamona Ct	G13
16	Gortnamona Hts	G13
25	Gortnamona Place	G13
16	Gortnamona Rise	G13
25	Gortnamona View	G13
25	Gortnamona Way	G13
19	Gotha Street	N12
31	Govan Drive	T12
42	Governor's Road	D22
19	Grace Avenue	P12
18	Grace Street	M12
11	*Gracehill Court	K10
	(Ardilea Street)	
37	Gracemount Park	N17
29	Graham Gardens	P13
42	Graham Gardens	D21
43	Graham Place	E21
43	Graham Street	E22
23	Graham's Bridge Road	V12
23	Grahamsbridge Park	V12
4	Grainon Way	L3
19	Grampian Avenue	P11
19	Grampian Close	P11
40	Grand Court	E20
19	Grand Parade	P12
22	Grand Prix Park	U12
40	Grand Street	E20
22	Grandprix Grove	U12
33	Grange Avenue	G16
2	Grange Lane	F3
33	Grange Park	G16
25	Grangeville Drive	H15
25	Grangeville Gdns	H15
23	Grangewood Ave	V11
23	Grangewood Cres	V11
23	Grangewood Glen	V11
23	Grangewood Gro	V11
22	Grangewood Hts	U11
23	Grangewood Hill	V11
23	Grangewood Lane	V11
22	Grangewood Manor	U11
22	Grangewood Park	U11
23	Grangewood Road	V11
22	Grangewood Tce	U11
25	Gransha Avenue	H13
25	Gransha Crescent	H13
25	Gransha Drive	H13
25	Gransha Gardens	H13
16	Gransha Green	H13
25	Gransha Grove	H13
22	Gransha Lane	U12
25	Gransha Parade	H13
25	Gransha Park	H13
25	Gransha Rise	H13
25	Gransha Road	U13
22	Gransha Walk	U12
25	Gransha Way	H13
21	Granton Park	T12
17	Granville Place	K12
11	Grasmere Gardens	K8
2	Gravelhill Road	G1
9	Graymount Cres	M6
9	Graymount Drive	M6
9	Graymount Gdns	L6

Page		Grid Ref
9	Graymount Grove	M6
9	Graymount Pde	M6
9	Graymount Park	M6
9	Graymount Road	M6
9	Graymount Tce	M6
9	Grays Court	M6
9	Gray's Lane	L6
44	Gray's Lane	S6
35	Gray's Park	L17
35	Gray's Park Ave	L17
35	Gray's Park Drive	L17
35	Gray's Park Gdns	L17
18	Great George's St	L10
27	Great Northern St	K13
18	Great Patrick St	M11
18	Great Victoria St	L12
20	Green Crescent	R12
7	Green End	M4
40	Green Hill	F19
40	Green Lane	F19
5	Green Link	P1
30	Green Mount	R13
32	Green Park	E18
20	Green Road	R12
7	Green Side	M4
7	Green Walk	M4
3	Greenacres	K2
25	Greenan	G14
25	Greenane Cres	G15
25	Greenane Drive	G15
43	Greenavon Mews	E22
39	Greenbank	D19
39	Greenburn Park	E19
32	Greenburn Way	E18
9	Greencastle Close	M6
9	Greencastle Place	M6
23	Greengraves Road	W12
3	Greenhill Gardens	K3
10	Greenhill Grove	H8
10	Greenhill Lane	H8
3	Greenhill Park	K3
3	Greenhill Road	K3
17	Greenland Street	L11
30	Greenlea Gardens	R13
43	Greenmount Gardens	E22
43	Greenmount Park	E22
12	Greenmount Pl	L10
12	Greenmount St	L10
19	Greenore Street	N12
34	Greenview Park	J16
19	Greenville Park	P12
19	*Greenville Court	P12
	(Greenville Road)	
19	Greenville Road	P12
19	Greenville Road	P12
19	Greenville Street	P12
29	Greenway	P14
43	Greenwood	E22
20	Greenwood Ave	R11
36	Greenwood Glen	M17
36	Greenwood Hill	M17
20	Greenwood Park	R11
36	Greer Park Ave	M17
36	Greer Park Drive	M17
36	Greer Park Hts	M17
43	Gregg Street	E21
43	Gregg Street Mews	E21
18	Greggs Quay	M11
18	Gresham Street	L11
3	Greyabbey Gdns	M1
30	Greycastle Manor	Q14
34	Greystown Ave	J16
34	Greystown Close	J16
34	Greystown Park	J16
29	Grillagh Way	N14
11	Groomsport Court	K10
11	Groomsport St	K10
17	*Grosvenor Court	K12
	(Roden Street)	
17	Grosvenor Road	K12
30	Grove Place	M9
43	Grove Street	E21
19	Grove Street East	P12
17	*Grove Tree North	K12
	(Devonshire Street)	
17	*Grove Tree South	K12
	(Devonshire Street)	

STREET INDEX

Page	Street	Grid Ref
18	Grovefield Place	N12
18	Grovefield Street	N12
43	Grovehill Avenue	E21
7	Gunnell Hill	L5
24	Gweedore Cres	F14
24	Gweedore Gdns	F14
24	Gweedore Park	N14
29	HADDINGTON GDNS	N13
39	Haddington Hill	C19
19	Haig Street	N12
19	Halcombe Street	N12
41	Halftown Road	A23
11	Halliday's Road	L9
11	Halliday's Road	L9
29	Halstein Drive	Q12
29	Hamel Court	P14
29	Hamel Drive	P14
29	Hamel Mews	P14
25	Hamill Glen	G14
25	Hamill Grove	G14
17	Hamill Street	L11
42	Hamilton Gardens	C21
19	Hamilton Road	N10
18	Hamilton Street	M12
5	Hampton Court	N1
44	Hampton Court	T7
5	Hampton Ct Mws	N1
28	Hampton Drive	M14
28	Hampton Garden	M14
28	Hampton Grove	L14
28	Hampton Manor	M15
28	Hampton Manor Drive	M15
28	Hampton Parade	M14
28	Hampton Park	M15
28	Hampton Place	M14
28	Hampton Strand	M14
43	Hancock Street	E21
12	Hanna Street	M10
24	Hannah Glen Hts	E14
24	Hannahstown Hill	E14
22	Hanwood Avenue	U12
22	Hanwood Court	U12
22	Hanwood Drive	U12
22	Hanwood Farm	U12
22	Hanwood Heights	U12
22	Hanwood Park	U12
27	Harberton Ave	J15
27	Harberton Drive	J15
27	Harberton Park	J15
11	Harcourt Drive	K9
32	Harcourt Terrace	F16
18	Hardcastle Street	L12
12	Hardinge Place	L10
19	Harkness Parade	P11
19	*Harland Close	N1
	(Harland Drive)	
19	Harland Drive	N1
19	Harland Park	P11
13	Harland Road	N10
19	Harland Walk	N11
28	Harleston Street	L14
3	Harmin Avenue	J3
3	Harmin Crescent	J3
3	Harmin Drive	J3
3	Harmin Parade	J3
3	Harmin Park	J3
10	Harmony Court	H9
40	Harmony Court	E20
40	Harmony Drive	E20
40	Harmony Hill	E20
40	Harmony Mews	E20
18	Harmony Street	L12
19	Harper Street	N11
33	Harris Crescent	F17
12	Harrisburg Street	M9
17	*Harrison Walk	K10
	(Danube Street)	
28	Harrow Street	M13
17	Harrowgate St	J12
11	Harrybrook St	K10
42	Harryville Park	D22
18	Hartington St	L12
12	Hartwell Place	L10
19	Harvey Court	N1
42	Haslem's Lane	D21
18	Hatfield Street	M13
19	Hatton Drive	N12
11	Havana Court	K9
11	Havana Gardens	K9
11	Havana Walk	K9
11	Havana Way	K9
18	Havelock Street	M12
24	Hawthorn Glen	E14
24	Hawthorn Glen	E14
24	Hawthorn Hill	E14
33	Hawthorn Park	F17
17	Hawthorn Street	K12
24	Hawthorn View	E14
20	Hawthornden Ct	R12
20	Hawthornden Dr	R11
20	Hawthornden	R11
	Gdns	
20	Hawthornden Lodge	R11
20	Hawthornden Mews	R11
20	Hawthornden Pk	R11
20	Hawthornden Rd	R11
20	Hawthornden Wy	R11
39	Hawthorne Lane	D20
4	Hawthorne Road	L1
18	Haymarket	L11
28	Haypark Avenue	M14
28	Haypark Gardens	M14
28	Haywood Avenue	M14
28	Haywood Drive	M14
33	Hazel Avenue	F18
10	Hazelbrook Drive	H8
3	Hazelburn Road	K1
42	Hazeldene Court	C21
42	Hazeldene Park	C21
6	Hazeldene Park	L5
17	Hazelfield Street	K10
24	Hazelwood Ave	F15
6	Hazelwood Park	L5
5	Heather Drive	M3
5	Heather Park	M3
11	Heather Street	J10
19	Heatherbell St	P12
11	Heathfield Court	K9
18	Hector Street	L11
21	Helen's Lea	S13
24	Helen's Wood	F15
20	Helgor Park	Q10
20	Helgor Park Mews	Q10
19	Hemp Street	P11
8	Henderson Ave	K8
11	Henderson Ave	K8
8	Henderson Court	K8
14	Henderson Court	R9
17	Henrietta Street	M12
17	Henry Place	L10
12	Henry Street	L10
28	Herat Street	M13
17	Herbert Street	J10
13	Herdman Channel Rd	N8
13	Herdman Channel Rd	N9
14	Heron Road	Q8
14	Heron View	Q8
41	Hertford Crescent	B22
42	Hertford Square	C22
10	Hesketh Gardens	J9
10	Hesketh Park	J9
10	Hesketh Road	J9
20	Hewitt Parade	K12
44	Hibernia Street	S6
16	High Gate	H11
16	High Green	H11
16	High Link	H11
16	High Pass	H11
16	High Side	H11
44	High Street	S6
18	High Street	M6
18	High Street	L11
18	High Street Ct	M11
16	High Way	H11
16	Highburn Cres	H11
16	Highburn Gardens	H11
11	Highbury Gardens	J9
16	Highcairn Drive	H11
16	Highcliff Gardens	H11
16	Highdene Gdns	H11
16	Highfern Gardens	H11
16	Highfield Drive	H11
39	Highfields Avenue	C19
39	Highfields Close	C19
39	Highfields Court	C19
39	Highfields Crescent	C19
39	Highfields Grove	C19
39	Highfields Park	C19
39	Highfields Road	C19
2	Highgate Close	F3
2	Highgate Drive	F3
2	Highgate Grove	F3
2	Highgate Manor	F3
16	Highgate Terrace	H11
16	Highland Parade	H11
16	Highpark Drive	H11
16	Highpark Cres	H11
16	Highpark Cross	H11
2	Hightown Ave	H3
6	Hightown Court	J3
6	Hightown Cres	J4
6	Hightown Drive	J4
6	Hightown Gdns	J4
6	Hightown Park	J4
6	Hightown Rise	J4
6	Hightown Road	J3
16	Highvale Gardens	H11
16	Highview Cresc	H11
40	Hilden Court	E20
40	Hilden Crescent	E20
40	Hilden Park	E20
40	Hilden Road	F20
40	Hilden View	F20
36	Hill Green	N17
18	Hill Street	D22
18	Hill Street	M11
33	Hill Street	G17
44	Hill Street Mews	S6
29	Hillburn Park	P14
39	Hillcrest	C20
4	Hillcrest Crescent	M2
4	Hillcrest Drive	M2
19	Hillcrest Gardens	Q12
4	Hillcrest Park	M2
19	Hillfoot Street	P11
43	Hillhall Close	E21
43	Hillhall Gardens	E21
43	Hillhall Park	E21
43	Hillhall Road	F21
25	Hillhead Avenue	G14
25	Hillhead Cottages	G14
25	Hillhead Court	G14
25	Hillhead Crescent	G15
25	Hillhead Drive	G15
25	Hillhead Heights	G14
25	Hillhead Park	G14
12	Hillman Close	L10
12	Hillman Court	L10
11	Hillman Street	L10
34	Hillmount	H16
34	Hillmount Gdns	H16
19	Hill's Avenue	P11
19	Hillsborough Dri	N13
19	Hillsborough Gdns	N13
42	Hillsborough Old Road	D22
19	Hillsborough Pde	P13
42	Hillsborough Road	C23
42	Hillsborough Road	D22
42	Hillside Court	C21
42	Hillside Crescent	C21
27	Hillside Crescent	L15
27	Hillside Drive	L15
27	Hillside Gardens	L15
42	Hillside Gardens	C21
4	Hillside Mews	M2
27	Hillside Park	L15
30	Hillside Park	Q14
3	Hillside View	M2
39	Hillview Avenue	E19
4	Hillview Avenue	M3
20	Hillview Avenue	Q12
40	Hillview Park	E19
5	Hillview Ave West	M3
11	Hillview Court	K10
3	Hillview Drive	J3
40	Hillview Gardens	E19
3	Hillview Park	J3
44	Hillview Place	T7
11	Hillview Road	K10
29	Hindsdale Park	P14
12	Hogarth Street	L10
43	Holborn Hall	F22
20	Holland Crescent	Q12
20	Holland Drive	Q12
20	Holland Gardens	Q12
20	Holland Park	Q12
3	Holly Lane	H2
5	Hollybank Court	M1
5	Hollybank Drive	M2
5	Hollybank Park	M2
5	Hollybank Way	N2
6	Hollybrook Avenue	
	(see insert)	
6	Hollybrook Crescent	
	(see insert)	
6	Hollybrook Court	
	(see insert)	
6	Hollybrook Gardens	
	(see insert)	
6	Hollybrook Grange	
	(see insert)	
6	Hollybrook Grove	
	(see insert)	
6	Hollybrook Heights	
	(see insert)	
6	Hollybrook Manor	
	(see insert)	
6	Hollybrook Park	
	(see insert)	
6	Hollybrook Road	
	(see insert)	
38	Hollyburn	B20
19	Hollycroft Ave	P12
33	Hollymount	F18
33	Hollymount	H16
34	Hollymount Court	H16
3	Hollyvale	K1
11	Holmdene Gdns	J9
18	*Holmes Court	M12
	(Market Street)	
18	Holmes Street	L12
10	Holylake Park	J8
27	Holyrood	L14
44	Holywood By-Pass	S7
14	Holywood Road	Q10
12	Hope Street	L12
20	Hopedene Court	Q11
20	Hopedene Mews	Q11
11	Hopefield Ave	L9
18	Hopefield Court	L8
17	Hopewell Avenue	K10
17	Hopewell Cres	L10
17	Hopewell Park	K10
17	Hopewell Square	L10
25	Horn Drive	F15
24	Horn Walk	F15
33	Hornbeam Road	F18
33	Hornbeam Walk	F18
11	Hornby Crescent	N11
19	Hornby Parade	N11
19	Hornby Street	N11
10	Horseshoe Court	H8
35	Hospital Road	L18
20	Houston Court	Q12
20	Houston Drive	Q13
20	Houston Gardens	Q13
20	Houston Park	Q13
2	Houston Road	G3
42	Howard Place	D21
18	Howard Street	L12
18	Howard St South	M12
17	Howe Street	K10
27	Hugh Street	K14
11	Hughenden Ave	K8
5	Hughes Court	N14
16	Hugo Street	J13
43	Huguenot Drive	E21
41	Hulls Lane	A22
19	Humber Court	N11
19	Humber Street	N11
19	Hunt Street	P11
11	Hunter Park	L12
28	Huntingdale	M15
18	*Hurst Park	L12
	(Linfield Avenue)	
17	Huss Court	K11

54

STREET INDEX

Page	Street	Grid Ref
17	Huss Row	K11
17	Hutchinson St	L12
2	Hydepark Close	G3
2	Hydepark Lane	F3
2	Hydepark Manor	F3
6	Hydepark Road (see insert)	
19	Hyndford Street	P12
12	**ILCHESTER STREET**	**L10**
19	Imperial Drive	N12
19	Imperial Street	N12
17	Ina Street	N11
23	Inchmarnock Drive	V12
11	India Street	L13
11	Indiana Avenue	K8
10	Ingledale Park	J9
14	Inglewood Court	Q10
42	Iniscarn Close	C21
42	Iniscarn Park	C21
25	Inishmore Cres	G14
34	Inishowen Drive	J16
7	Innis Avenue	M4
44	Innis Court	S6
39	Innis Gardens	D20
7	Innis Park	M4
7	Innis Walk	M4
4	Inniscarn Drive	M3
3	Inniscoole Park	J3
9	Innisfayle Drive	L7
9	Innisfayle Gardens	L7
42	Innisfayle Park	C21
9	Innisfayle Park	L7
9	Innisfayle Pass	L7
42	Innisfayle Road	C21
9	Innisfayle Road	L7
7	Innisrush Gardens	M4
17	Institution Place	L11
11	Inver Avenue	K8
44	Inver Park	T7
14	Inverary Avenue	Q10
14	Inverary Drive	Q10
7	Inveresk Park	M4
14	Inverleith Drive	Q10
14	Invernook Drive	Q10
14	Invernook Park	Q10
14	Inverwood Court	Q10
14	Inverwood Gdns	Q10
7	Iona Gardens	M4
7	Iona Park	M4
17	Ireton Street	L12
17	Iris Close	J12
17	Iris Court	J12
17	Iris Drive	J12
	(Ceide na Seileastar)	
17	Iris Grove	J12
24	Iris Link	E17
17	Iris Mews	J12
17	Iris Street	J12
17	Iris Walk	J12
17	Irwell Court	J12
19	Irwin Avenue	P11
19	Irwin Cresent	Q11
19	Irwin Drive	P11
17	Isaac's Court	L12
16	Isadore Avenue	J11
17	Island Street	N11
17	Islandbawn Drive	J12
17	Islandbawn Street	J12
38	Islandkelly Park	B19
23	Islay Gardens	V12
19	Isoline Street	P12
19	Isthmus Street	N12
42	Ivan Street	D12
12	Ivan Street	M9
17	Iveagh Cresent	J12
17	Iveagh Drive	J12
17	Iveagh Parade	J12
17	Iveagh Street	J12
17	Iverna Close	K12
17	Iverna Street	K12
44	**JACKSON'S RD**	**S7**
11	Jaffa Street	K10
11	Jamaica Court	J9
11	Jamaica Road	K9
11	Jamaica Street	J9
11	Jamaica Way	K9
11	James Court	L8
38	James Craig Way	B20
18	James St South	L12
28	Jameson Street	M14
32	Jasmine Corner	E16
32	Jasmine End	E16
32	Jasmine Walk	E16
32	Jasmine Way	E16
12	Jellicoe Avenue	L9
12	Jellicoe Drive	L8
12	Jellicoe Park	L8
12	Jellicoe Parade	L8
5	Jennings Drive	M1
5	Jennings Park	M1
12	Jennymount St	M9
17	Jeremy Walk	D22
39	Jersey Avenue	D20
17	Jersey Place	K10
28	Jerusalem Street	M13
11	Joanmount Drive	J8
11	Joanmount Gdns	J8
11	Joanmount Park	J8
19	Jocelyn Avenue	N12
19	Jocelyn Gardens	N12
19	Jocelyn Street	N12
17	John Street	L11
38	Johnson Way	B20
20	Johnston Court	R12
19	Jonesboro Park	P12
19	Jonesboro Park	N12
5	Jordanstown Ave	P2
5	Jordanstown Hts	N1
5	Jordanstown Mws	N1
5	Jordanstown Rise	N1
5	Jordanstown Rd	N1
18	Joy Street	M12
18	Joy Street	M12
17	Joy's Entry	M11
42	Jubilee Avenue	C22
11	Jubilee Avenue	L9
42	Jubilee Place	C22
18	Jubilee Road	K13
17	Jude Street	K11
19	Julia Street	P11
32	Juniper Court	E17
32	Juniper Park	E17
32	Juniper Rise	E17
32	Juniper Square	E17
32	Juniper Way	E17
11	**KANSAS AVE FLATS**	**L8**
11	Kansas Avenue	K8
23	Karrington Hts	V13
17	Kashmir Road	J11
19	Kathleen Court	N11
34	Katrine Park	H16
10	Keadyville Ave	M9
19	Keatley Street	N11
42	Keightley Court	D22
35	Kells Avenue	F15
11	Kelvin Parade	K9
25	Kenard Avenue	G14
19	Kenbaan Court	N12
19	Kenbaan Street	N12
11	Kenbella Parade	L8
17	Kendal Street	K11
39	Kenilworth Avenue	C19
39	Kenilworth Drive	C19
39	Kenilworth Grove	C19
39	Kenilworth Mews	C19
39	Kenilworth Park	C19
19	*Kenilworth Place	N11
	(Ballymacarrett Road)	
17	Kenmare Park	L12
23	Kenmore Park	V12
23	Kenmore Walk	V12
39	Kennedy Drive	D19
25	Kennedy Way	H13
17	Kennel Bridge	R9
19	Kensington Ave	P12
20	Kensington Court	R12
20	Kensington Cres	R12
21	Kensington Drive	S12
20	Kensington Gdns Sth	R13
20	Kensington Gdns	R13
20	Kensington Gdns West	R13
20	Kensington Gate	R12
21	Kensington Manor	S13
43	Kensington Park	E22
20	Kensington Park	R13
20	Kensington Road	R13
21	Kensington Road	S13
17	Kensington St	L12
18	Kent Street	L11
7	Kernan Drive	L5
12	Kerrera Court	J10
11	Kerrera Mews	J10
11	Kerrera Street	J10
20	Kerrsland Cres	Q12
20	Kerrsland Drive	Q12
20	Kerrsland Mews	Q12
20	Kerrsland Parade	Q12
24	Kerrykeel Gardens	F14
37	Kerrymount Ave	N16
24	Kestrel Grange	F15
17	Keswick Street	K10
36	Kew Gardens	N17
18	Keyland's Place	L12
23	Kilberry Park	W12
24	Kilbourne Park	F15
29	Kilbroney Bend	P14
17	Kilburn Street	K13
8	Kilcoole Gardens	S7
11	Kilcoole Park	K8
8	Kilcoole Park	S7
17	Kildare Street	L11
	(Sraid Chill Dara)	
20	Kilhorne Gardens	R13
29	Killagan Bend	P14
42	Killaney Avenue	C22
42	Killaney Court	C22
34	Killard Place	H16
30	Killarn Close	Q13
32	Killeaton Cres	E18
32	Killeaton Gardens	E18
32	Killeaton Park	E18
25	Killen Park	G14
17	Killen Street	L11
39	Killowen Crescent	C20
38	Killowen Grange	B19
38	Killowen Mews	B20
39	Killowen Park	C20
19	Killowen Street	N12
7	Killowen Terrace	M3
35	Killynether Gdns	L17
35	Killynether Walk	L17
31	Kilmakee Park	T13
17	Kilmore Close	K11
17	Kilmore Square	K11
21	Kilmory Gardens	T12
23	Kilmuir Avenue	V12
2	Kiln Road	H1
17	Kilronan Street	L10
35	Kilwarlin Crescent	L17
35	Kilwarlin Walk	L17
28	Kimberley Drive	M14
3	Kimberley Drive	K2
3	Kimberley Park	K2
3	Kimberley Road	K2
28	Kimberley Street	M14
19	Kimona Drive	P11
19	Kimona Street	P11
28	Kinallen Court	M13
28	Kinallen Street	M13
34	Kinbane Way	H16
20	Kincora Avenue	Q11
21	Kincraig Avenue	T12
6	Kincraig Park	L5
20	Kinedar Cresent	R11
17	King Street Mews	L11
17	King Street	L11
4	King's Avenue	M2
21	King's Brae	S12
26	Kings Court	J15
20	King's Cresent	R12
5	King's Cresent	M2
5	Kings Court	M2
5	King's Drive	M2
20	King's Drive	R12
5	King's Gardens	M3
21	King's Link	S12
21	Kings Manor	S12
5	King's Parade	M2
20	King's Park	R12
4	King's Road	M2
20	King's Road	R12
21	King's Road	S12
21	King's Square	S12
5	King's Terrace	M2
20	Kings Vale	R12
5	Kings Walk	N3
5	King's Way	M2
29	Kingsberry Park	N14
19	*Kingscourt Ave	N12
	(Kingscourt Street)	
19	Kingscourt Close	N12
19	Kingscourt Cres	N12
19	Kingscourt Street	N12
21	Kingsdale Park	S12
21	Kingsden Park	R12
21	Kingsland Drive	S12
21	Kingsland Park	S12
20	Kingsleigh	R12
11	Kingsley Court	Q11
11	Kingsmere Ave	K9
11	Kingston Court	K9
33	Kingsway	F17
21	Kingsway Avenue	S12
21	Kingsway Close	S12
21	Kingsway Drive	S12
21	Kingsway Gardens	S12
21	Kingsway Park	S12
21	Kingswood Park	S12
19	Kingswood Street	N12
11	Kinnaird Close	L10
11	Kinnaird Place	L10
11	Kinnaird Street	L10
11	Kinnaird Terrace	L10
44	Kinnegar Avenue	S7
44	Kinnegar Court	S7
44	Kinnegar Drive	S7
34	Kinnegar Road	H16
44	Kinnegar Road	S6
12	Kinross Avenue	T12
17	Kirk Street	J11
35	Kirkistown Ave	L17
35	Kirkistown Walk	L17
20	Kirkliston Drive	Q12
20	Kirkliston Gardens	Q12
20	Kirkliston Park	Q12
25	Kirkview Drive	H16
39	Kirkwoods Park	D19
39	Kirkwoods Road	D19
21	Kirn Park	T12
17	Kitchener Drive	K13
17	Kitchener Street	K13
17	Klondyke Street	K10
29	Knights Green	P13
38	Knightsbridge	B19
27	Knightsbridge Manor	L15
27	Knightsbridge Mews	L15
27	Knightsbridge Pk	L15
20	Knock Green	R13
20	Knock Grove	Q13
20	Knock Link	R13
20	Knock Road	R13
20	Knock Way	R13
42	Knockagh Road	C21
4	Knockane Way	M3
37	Knockbracken Manor	P17
37	Knockbracken Pk	N15
37	Knockbracken Rd	Q17
29	Knockbracken Q18 Road South	
28	Knockbreda Drive	N15
29	Knockbreda Gdns	N15
28	Knockbreda Park	N15
29	Knockbreda Park	N15
28	Knockbreda Pk Mews	N14
29	Knockbreda Road	N14
29	Knockbreda Road	N14
41	Knockburn Avenue	B21
41	Knockburn Close	B21
41	Knockburn Court	B21
41	Knockburn Crescent	B21
41	Knockburn Drive	B21
41	Knockburn Gardens	B21

STREET INDEX

Page	Street	Grid Ref
41	Knockburn Grove	B21
41	Knockburn Park	B21
21	Knockburn Park	S12
20	Knockcastle Park	R12
41	Knockdarragh Park	B21
21	Knockdarragh Park	S10
20	Knockdene Park	R12
20	Knockdene Pk Nth	R12
20	Knockdene Pk Sth	R12
25	Knockdhu Park	G14
29	Knockeden Cres	N14
29	Knockeden Drive	N14
29	Knockeden Grove	N14
29	Knockeden Pde	N14
29	Knockeden Park	N14
4	Knockenagh Ave	M3
4	Knockenagh Walk	M3
20	Knockhill Park	R12
21	Knockland Park	S12
20	Knocklofty Court	R11
20	Knocklofty Park	R11
21	Knockmarloch Pk	S10
41	Knockmore Park	B21
41	Knockmore Road	B21
42	Knockmore Square	C22
20	Knockmount Gdns	R13
20	Knockmount Park	R13
14	Knocknagoney Ave	R9
14	Knocknagoney Dale	R9
14	Knocknagoney Drive	R9
14	Knocknagoney Gdns	R9
14	Knocknagoney Green	R9
14	Knocknagoney Grove	R9
14	Knocknagoney Pk	R9
14	Knocknagoney Rd	R9
14	Knocknagoney Way	R9
4	Knockreagh Gdns	M3
20	Knocktern Gdns	R11
20	Knockvale Grove	R12
20	Knockvale Park	R12
4	Knockview Ave	L1
4	Knockview Cres	L1
4	Knockview Drive	L1
4	Knockview Gdns	L1
4	Knockview Manor	L1
4	Knockview Park	L1
4	Knockview Road	L1
20	Knockwood Cres	Q13
20	Knockwood Drive	Q13
20	Knockwood Grove	Q13
20	Knockwood Park	Q13
9	Knutstord Drive	K9
25	Koram Ring	H14
19	Kyle Street	P11
4	Kylemore Bend	M3
11	Kylemore Park	K8
17	LA SALLE DRIVE	J12
17	La Salle Gardens	J12
17	La Salle Mews	J12
16	La Salle Park	J12
19	Laburnum Court	P11
32	Laburnum Green	E17
19	Laburnum Lane	P11
32	Laburnum Park	E17
32	*Laburnum Row	F16
	(Laburnum Way)	
19	Laburnum Street	P11
32	Laburnum Walk	E17
32	Laburnum Way	F16
32	*Lackagh Court	N11
	(Ballymacarrett Road)	
4	Lacken Gardens	M3
4	Lacken Walk	M3
29	Ladas Drive	P13
29	Ladas Walk	P13
29	Ladas Way	P13
19	Ladbrook Drive	J10
17	Lady Street	K11
25	Ladybrook Ave	G15
25	Ladybrook Cres	G15
25	Ladybrook Cross	G15
25	Ladybrook Drive	G15
25	Ladybrook Gdns	G15
25	Ladybrook Grove	G15
25	Ladybrook Parade	G15
25	Ladybrook Park	G15
25	Ladybrook Park	G15
5	Ladye Park	M1
17	*Ladymar Court	K12
	(Marchioness Street)	
17	*Ladymar Grove	K12
	(Marchioness Street)	
17	*Ladymar Park	K12
	(Marchioness Street)	
17	*Ladymar Walk	K12
	(Marchioness Street)	
3	Ladysmith Lane	J2
42	Lagan Walk	C22
42	Laganbank Road	M11
42	Laganbank Road	D21
28	Laganvale Court	L14
28	Laganvale Manor	L15
28	Laganvale Street	L14
42	Laganview	D22
18	Laganview Court	M11
18	Laganview Mews	M11
32	Lagmore Avenue	D16
32	Lagmore Dale	E17
32	Lagmore Downs	E17
32	Lagmore Drive	E17
32	Lagmore Grove	E17
32	Lagmore Meadows	E17
32	LagmoreMeadows	E16
32	Lagmore Road	D16
32	Lagmore View	D16
25	Lake Glen Ave	H13
25	Lake Glen Close	H13
25	Lake Glen Cres	H13
25	Lake Glen Drive	H13
25	Lake Glen Green	H13
25	Lake Glen Parade	H13
25	Lake Glen Park	H13
34	Lakeside Drive	H17
3	Lakeview Avenue	K1
3	Lakeview Gardens	K1
3	Lakeview Grove	K1
3	Lakeview Park	K1
40	Lambeg Road	E19
23	Lambert Avenue	V11
23	Lambert Avenue	V11
23	Lambert Glen	V11
23	Lambert Park	V11
23	Lambert Rise	V11
18	Lanark Way	J11
18	Lancaster Street	L10
18	Lancaster Terrace	L10
29	Lancedean Road	P14
27	Lancefield Road	K14
43	Landor Park	E22
11	Landscape Tce	K10
28	Landseer Street	L13
11	Langley Street	K10
19	Langtry Court	N11
9	Lansdowne Drive	L7
9	Lansdowne Mews	L7
9	Lansdowne Park	L7
43	Lansdowne Park	E22
9	Lansdowne Pk Nth	L7
9	Lansdowne Road	L7
7	Lanyon Place	M12
7	Laragh Court	L5
44	Larch Close	S7
33	Larch Grove	G18
3	Larch Grove	K1
33	Larch Hill	G18
43	Largymore Drive	E22
43	Largymore Link	E22
33	Larkfield Avenue	G16
14	Larkfield Court	Q10
14	Larkfield Drive	Q10
19	Larkfield Gardens	P10
19	Larkfield Grove	Q10
19	Larkfield Manor	P10
19	Larkfield Park	Q10
19	Larkfield Road	P10
24	Larkspur Rise	F14
27	Larkstone Street	J14
9	Laundry Lane	J4
39	Laurel Grove	C20
32	Laurel Park	E17
33	Laurel Way	F17
28	Laurel Wood	M15
24	Laurelbank	E16
37	Laurelgrove Ave	P17
37	Laurelgrove Ct	P17
37	Laurelgrove Cres	P17
37	Laurelgrove Dale	P17
37	Laurelgrove Manor	P17
37	Laurelgrove Park	P17
39	Laurelhill Park	C20
39	Laurelhill Road	C20
20	Laurelvale	R11
18	Lavens Drive	H9
17	Lawnbrook Ave	K11
17	Lawnbrook Drive	K11
40	Lawnbrook Drive	E20
17	Lawnbrook Sq	K11
40	Lawnmount Crescent	E20
19	Lawnmount St	N12
18	Lawnview Street	J10
18	Lawrence Street	L13
12	Law's Court	L11
9	Lawther Court	L9
19	Lawyer Gardens	L12
30	Lead Hill	Q14
30	Lead Hill Park	Q14
30	Lead Hill View	Q14
40	Leamington Place	E21
18	Lecale Street	K13
25	Leestone Terrace	F15
10	Legann Street	H9
10	Leganoe Street	H8
10	Leggagh Court	H8
10	Leginn Street	H8
10	Legmail Street	H9
10	Legnavea Place	H8
19	Leitrim Street	N12
19	Lelia Street	N11
17	Lemberg Street	K12
44	Lemonfield Ave	T7
19	Lena Street	P11
4	Lenaderg Terrace	M3
25	Lenadoon Ave	F15
24	Lenadoon Ave	F14
25	Lenadoon Walk	F15
36	Lenaghan Ave	N17
36	Lenaghan Court	N16
36	Lenaghan Cres	N16
36	Lenaghan Gdns	N16
36	Lenaghan Park	N16
5	Lenamore Ave	N1
5	Lenamore Cres	N1
5	Lenamore Drive	N1
5	Lenamore Gdns	N1
5	Lenamore Park	N1
39	Lenamore Park	D20
19	Lendrick Street	N11
36	Lennox Avenue	N16
27	Lennoxvale	L13
27	Lenwood Drive	G17
39	Lenwood Hill	C20
17	Leopold Gardens	J10
17	Leopold Park	J10
11	Leopold Place	J10
17	Leopold Street	K10
17	Leopold Street	J10
17	Leoville Street	J11
15	Lepper Street	L10
10	Leroy Street	H9
17	Lesley Villas	K14
39	Lester Avenue	D20
19	Lester Street	H8
19	Lewis Court	N12
39	Leydene Court	C20
20	Library Court	Q11
18	Library Street	L11
18	Lichfield Avenue	P12
11	Liffey Court	K10
10	Ligoniel Place	H8
10	Ligoniel Road	H8
33	Lilac Grove	F18
38	Lillie Court	B20
25	Lille Park	H16
12	Lilliput Court	M10
10	Lime Court	L11
10	Limehill Grove	H8
43	Limehill Road	E23
10	Limehill Street	H8
43	Limehurst Way	E21
10	Limepark Mews	H9
11	Limestone Road	L9
38	Limetree Avenue	B20
38	Limetree Lodge	B20
38	Limetree Meadow	B20
20	Limewood Grove	R11
11	Lincoln Avenue	L10
17	Lincoln Place	L12
17	Lincoln Square	K12
17	Linden Gardens	K9
17	Linden Street	K11
33	Linden Walk	G18
18	Lindsay Court	L12
18	Lindsay Street	L12
18	Lindsay Way	L12
40	Linen Court	F20
18	Linen Grove	H8
18	Linen Hall Street	L12
18	Linen Hall St West	L12
42	Linenhall Street	D21
17	Linfield Avenue	L12
17	*Linfield Drive	L12
	(Linfield Road)	
17	Linfield Gardens	L12
17	Linfield Road	L12
4	Linford Green	M3
34	Linkview Park	J16
39	Linnet Park	C20
17	*Linview Court	K12
	(Roden Street)	
19	Lisavon Drive	P10
19	Lisavon Parade	P11
19	Lisavon Street	P11
4	Lisbane Avenue	M1
4	Lisbane Drive	M1
4	Lisbane Gardens	M1
18	Lisbon Street	N11
9	Lisbreen Park	L8
27	Lisburn Avenue	K14
42	Lisburn Leisure Pk	D2
27	Lisburn Road	K14
42	Lisburn Square	D21
3	Liscoole Park	K3
8	Lisdarragh Park	K7
17	Lisfaddan Cres	K11
17	Lisfaddan Drive	L11
17	Lisfaddan Place	L11
17	Lisfaddan Way	L11
27	Lislea Avenue	J14
27	Lislea Drive	J14
31	Lisleen Road	T15
31	Lisleen Road East	T15
19	Lismain Street	N13
5	Lismara Court	N4
23	Lismore Drive	W12
19	Lismore Street	N12
23	Lismore Way	W12
8	Lismoyne Park	K7
30	Lisnabreeny Road	Q15
30	Lisnabreeny Rd East	Q15
39	Lisnagarvey Crescent	D20
39	Lisnagarvey Drive	D20
30	Lisnasharragh Pk	Q14
30	Lisnasharragh Tce	Q14
42	Lisnoe Walk	C22
29	Lissan Close	N14
29	Lissan Link	N14
42	Lissue Crescent	C22
41	Lissue Road	A22
41	Lissue Walk	A22
17	Lisvarna Heights	K11
17	Lisvarna Place	K12
18	Little Charlotte St	M12
18	Little Corporation St	M10
18	Little Donegall St	L11
18	*Little Edward St	L11
	(Edward Street)	
18	Little George's St	L10
18	Little May Street	M12

STREET INDEX

Page	Street	Grid Ref
18	Little Patrick St	M11
18	Little Victoria St	L12
18	Little York Street	L11
43	Llewellyn Avenue	E21
40	Llewellyn Court	E21
40	Llewellyn Drive	E21
17	Locan Street	J12
21	Lochinver Drive	T13
26	Lockside Court	L14
26	Locksley Drive	H15
34	Locksley Gardens	H16
26	Locksley Grange	H15
26	Locksley Lane	H15
34	Locksley Parade	H16
34	Locksley Park	H16
34	Locksley Place	H16
28	Lockview Road	L14
38	Lombard Avenue	C20
38	Lombard Park	C20
18	Lombard Street	L11
19	Lomond Avenue	P11
19	Lomond Street	P11
18	London Road	N12
18	London Street	N12
28	Long Acre	N15
7	Longlands Ave	L5
7	Longlands Court	L5
7	Longlands Park	L5
7	Longlands Road	L5
7	Longlands Walk	L5
23	Longstone Ave	V12
23	Longstone Close	V12
23	Longstone Court	V12
23	Longstone Cres	V12
23	Longstone Drive	V12
23	Longstone Green	V12
23	Longstone Mews	V12
42	Longstone Street	C21
23	Longstone Way	V12
7	Longwood Road	M5
19	Loopland Cres	P13
19	Loopland Court	P13
19	Loopland Drive	P13
29	Loopland Gardens	P13
19	Loopland Grove	P13
19	Loopland Parade	P13
19	Loopland Park	P13
19	Loopland Road	P13
19	Lord Street	N12
17	Lorne Street	K13
11	Lothair Avenue	L9
21	Lothian Avenue	T12
18	Louden Street	L11
18	Lough Lea	N11
	(Loch Lao)	
5	Loughgall Gdns	N2
4	Loughmoney Park	M3
11	Loughrey Court	L9
19	Loughview	J7
44	Loughview Ave	S7
29	Loughview Drive	N15
8	Loughview Manor	J7
10	Loughview St	H9
12	Loughview Tce	M9
11	Louisa Court	K9
19	Lovatt Street	P12
43	Low Road	E21
30	Lower Braniel Rd	R14
21	Lower Clonard Street	K11
18	Lower Crescent	L12
17	Lower Garfield St	L11
17	Lower Kilburn St	K11
18	Lower Regent St	L10
17	Lower Rockview St	K12
18	Lower Stanfield St	M12
27	Lower Windsor Ave	K13
21	Lowland Avenue	T12
21	Lowland Gardens	T12
21	Lowland Walk	T12
28	Lowry Court	M15
9	Lowwood Gdns	L7
9	Lowwood Park	L7
28	Lucerne Parade	L4
17	Lucknow Street	J11
12	Ludlow Square	L10
10	Lupus Grove	H8
19	Luxor Gardens	P12
17	Lyle Court	K10
33	Lyme Court	G17
5	Lynda Avenue	N1
5	Lynda Crescent	N2
5	Lynda Farm	N1
5	Lynda Gardens	N1
5	Lynda Meadows	N2
3	Lyndale Court	H2
16	Lyndhurst Ave	H10
16	Lyndhurst Close	H10
16	Lyndhurst Cres	H10
16	Lyndhurst Court	H10
16	Lyndhurst Drive	H10
16	Lyndhurst Gdns	H10
16	Lyndhurst Grove	H10
16	Lyndhurst Hts	H10
16	Lyndhurst Link	H10
16	Lyndhurst Meadows	H10
16	Lyndhurst Parade	H10
16	Lyndhurst Park	H10
16	Lyndhurst Path	H10
16	Lyndhurst Place	H10
16	Lyndhurst Rise	H10
16	Lyndhurst Row	H10
16	Lyndhurst View	H10
16	Lyndhurst View Ave	H10
16	Lyndhurst View Close	H10
16	Lyndhurst View Park	H10
16	Lyndhurst View Road	H10
16	Lyndhurst Walk	H10
16	Lyndhurst Way	H10
44	Lynwood Park	T7
25	M1 MOTORWAY	H14
3	M2 Motorway	H3
6	M2 Motorway	K4
12	M2 Motorway	M8
7	M5 Motorway	N5
18	Mabel Court	L12
12	Mackey Street	L9
11	Madison Avenue	K8
19	Madison Ave East	P11
17	Madras Street	K10
18	Madrid Court	N11
18	Madrid Street	N11
18	Magdala Street	L13
8	Magee's Lane	L10
39	Magheralave Court	D19
39	Magheralave Grange	D19
39	Magheralave Manor	D19
39	Magheralave Park East	D20
39	Magheralave Park North	D20
39	Magheralave Park South	D20
42	Magheralave Road	D21
19	Maghies Place	N12
32	Magnolia Park	E17
35	Mahee Close	L17
17	Majestic Drive	L12
17	Major Street	N11
17	Malcomson Street	K12
17	Maldon Street	K12
34	Malfin Court	J16
34	Malfin Drive	J16
25	Malinmore Park	F15
2	Mallusk Drive	H3
2	Mallusk Road	F2
27	Malone Avenue	L13
27	Malone Beeches	K15
27	Malone Chase	L13
27	Malone Court	K15
27	Malone Ct Mews	K15
27	Malone Gardens	G17
27	Malone Grange	K15
34	Malone Heights	J17
34	Malone Hill Park	K15
27	Malone Manor	K15
35	Malone Meadows	K16
27	Malone Park	J15
27	Malone Pk Central	K15
27	Malone Park Lane	J15
17	Malone Place	L12
27	Malone Road	K14
35	Malone Valley Park	K16
34	Malone View Ave	J17
34	Malone View Cres	J16
34	Malone View Park	J16
34	Malone View Park	J17
34	Malone View Road	J17
39	Malory Gardens	C19
34	Malton Court	J16
34	Malton Drive	J16
34	Malton Rise	J16
34	Malton Vale	J16
17	Malvern Close	K10
17	Malvern Street	K11
17	Malvern Way	K11
17	Malvern Way	K10
34	Malwood Close	J16
34	Malwood Park	J16
19	Manderson Street	P11
43	Mandeville Avenue	E21
19	Manna Grove	P13
31	Mann's Road	T15
11	Manor Close	K10
11	Manor Court	K10
11	Manor Drive	K10
42	Manor Drive	D22
33	Manor Mews	G16
42	Manor Park	D22
11	Manor Street	K10
11	Manor Street	K10
3	Manse Court	J1
3	Manse Drive	J1
3	Manse Green	Jl
3	Manse Rise	Jl
3	Manse Road	K1
30	Manse Road	Q15
3	Manse Terrace	J1
3	Manse Walk	Jl
3	Manse Way	Jl
17	Mansfield Street	K11
33	Maple Crescent	G18
44	Maple Court	S7
42	Maralin Avenue	C22
11	Maralin Place	L10
17	March Street	J11
17	Marchioness Green	K12
17	Marchioness St	K12
18	Marcus Ward St	L12
24	Margaretta Court	F15
24	Margaretta Crescent	F15
24	Margaretta Park	F15
26	Marguerite Park	H15
30	Marina Park	Q13
5	Marine Court	N3
44	Marine Parade	S6
12	Marine Street	M10
44	Marino Park	T6
44	Marino Road	T6
42	Market Lane	D21
42	Market Place	D21
18	Market Square	D21
18	Market Street	M12
18	Market Street	M12
42	Market Street	D21
27	Marlborough Ave	K14
27	Marlborough Ct	K14
27	Marlborough Gate	K14
27	Marlborough Gdns	K14
30	Marlborough Hts	Q14
27	Marlborough Manor	K14
27	Marlborough Park	K14
27	Marlborough Park	K14
27	Marlborough Pk Cent	K14
27	Marlborough Pk East	K14
	Cross Avenue	
27	Marlborough Pk Nth	K14
27	Marlborough Pk Sth	K14
18	Marlborough St	M11
31	Marlfield Drive	S13
31	Marlfield Rise	S13
31	Marmont Cres	S13
17	Marmont Drive	R10
14	Marmont Park	R10
20	Marmount Gdns	J8
39	Marnabrae	D19
39	Marnabrae Park	D19
18	Marquis Street	L11
11	Marsden Gardens	L9
30	Marshalls Road	Q13
7	Martin Park	N4
19	Martin Street	N11
19	Martinez Avenue	P12
36	Marvinville Park	N17
28	Marylebone Park	L15
27	Maryville Avenue	K14
18	Maryville Court	L12
27	Maryville Park	K15
18	Maryville Street	L12
20	Mashona Court	N12
21	Massey Avenue	S10
21	Massey Court	S11
21	Massey Green	S10
21	Massey Park	S10
17	Matchet Street	K10
17	Matilda Avenue	L12
17	Matilda Drive	L12
17	Matilda Gardens	L12
22	Mawhinney Park	U12
17	Maxwell Street	L12
27	Maxwell's Place	L12
18	May Street	M12
29	Mayfair Avenue	P13
11	*Mayfair Court	K10
	(Ardilea Street)	
6	Mayfield Drive	
	(see insert)	
6	Mayfield Gardens	
	(see insert)	
6	Mayfield Heights	
	(see insert)	
6	Mayfield Park	
	(see insert)	
6	Mayfield Road	
	(see insert)	
25	Mayfield Square	G15
27	Mayfield Street	K14
6	Mayfield Village	
	(see insert)	
39	Mayfields	D19
29	Mayflower Street	P12
19	Maymount Street	N12
17	Mayo Court	J11
17	Mayo Link	J11
17	Mayo Park	J11
17	Mayo Place	J11
17	Mayo Street	J11
18	Mays Meadows	M12
42	Maze Park	C22
17	McAllister Court	P1
17	McAdam Gardens	L12
17	McAdam Park	L12
19	McArthur Court	N11
19	*McAtamney Tce	N11
	(Mountpottinger Road)	
18	McAuley Park	M12
11	McCandless St	K10
29	McCaughan Park	P14
13	McCaughey Road	N9
11	McCavana's Place	L12
18	McCleery Street	L10
18	McClintock Street	L12
18	McClure Street	L12
18	McDonnell Court	K12
17	McDonnell Street	K12
18	Mclvors Place	L11
42	McKeown Street	D21
18	McKibben's Court	L11
32	McKinstry Road	E18
19	McMaster Street	N11
18	McMullan's Lane	N12
17	McQuillan Street	K12
12	Meadow Close	L10
12	Meadow Place	L10
5	Meadowbank	P1
5	Meadowbank Ct	P1
5	Meadowbank Lane	P1
5	Meadowbank Park	M1
22	Meadowbank Park	U12
27	Meadowbank Pl	K13
27	Meadowbank St	K13
10	Meadowhill	F14
24	Meadowhill Grange	F14
10	Meadowhill View	F14
5	Meadowlands	P1
24	Meadowvale	D23
19	Medway Court	N11
19	Medway Street	N11
19	Meekon Street	P11

STREET INDEX

Page	Street	Grid Ref
43	Meeting House Lane	F21
17	Melbourne Street	L11
21	Melfort Drive	S12
21	Melfort Terrace	T12
32	Melmore Drive	E18
19	Melrose Avenue	P12
27	Melrose Street	K13
43	Mercer Court	E21
43	Mercer Street	E21
41	Meridi Street	K12
17	Merkland Place	J11
29	Merok Crescent	P14
29	Merok Drive	P14
29	Merok Gardens	P14
29	Merok Park	P14
24	Merrion Park	F15
14	Merryfield Drive	K7
19	Mersey Street	P11
9	Merston Gardens	L6
7	Merville Mews	M5
12	Mervue Court	L10
12	Mervue Street	L10
11	Meyrick Park	J8
16	Mica Drive	J12
16	Mica Street	J12
2	Michelin Road	H3
31	Middle Braniel Rd	S14
38	Middlepath St	M11
12	Midland Close	M10
12	Midland Crescent	M10
12	Midland Terrace	M10
12	Mileriver Street	L9
3	Milewater Close	J1
3	Milewater Court	J1
3	Milewater Drive	J1
12	Milewater Road	M9
12	Milewater Street	M9
3	Milewater Terrace	J1
3	Milewater Way	J1
17	*Milford Close	K11
	(Milford Place)	
17	Milford Place	K11
17	Milford Rise	L11
17	Milford Street	L11
33	Milfort Avenue	G17
33	Milfort Terrace	G17
10	Mill Avenue	G8
2	Mill Grange	F3
19	Mill Pond Court	P12
7	Mill Road	M5
37	Mill Road	N18
36	Mill Road West	N18
40	Mill Street	E20
11	Mill Street West	K10
23	Millar Street	N13
23	Millar's Close	V12
23	Millar's Court	V12
23	Millar's Crescent	V12
23	Millar's Drive	V12
23	Millar's Forge	V13
23	Millar's Grove	V12
23	Millar's Lane	V12
23	Millar's Park	V12
23	Millar's View	V13
10	Millbank Park	H8
43	Millbrook Road	E21
43	Millbrook Walk	E21
35	Millburn Court	K15
16	Millennium Way	J12
13	Millfield	L11
23	Millmount Road	W13
32	Milltown Avenue	D18
32	Milltown Close	D18
35	Milltown Hill	L17
32	Milltown Park	D18
32	Milltown Road	K17
32	Milltown Row	J13
10	Millview Court	H8
17	Milner Street	K15
23	Minard Park	V12
13	Mind's Way	L13
12	Mineral Street	M9
35	Minnowburn Drive	L17
35	Minnowburn Gdns	L17
35	Minnowburn Mews	L17
35	Minnowburn Tce	L17
25	Mizen Gardens	F14
22	Moatview Cres	U12
22	Moatview Park	U12
18	Moffatt Street	L10
18	Moira Court	N11
	(Cuirt Mhaigh Rath)	
41	Moira Park	B21
41	Moira Road	A22
42	Moira Road	E22
17	Moltke Street	K13
38	Molyneaux Road	B20
18	Molyneaux Street	M10
38	Molyneaux Walk	B20
16	Monagh By-Pass	G13
16	Monagh Crescent	G13
16	Monagh Drive	G12
16	Monagh Grove	G13
16	Monagh Link	G13
16	Monagh Parade	G12
16	Monagh Road	G13
17	Monarch Parade	K12
17	Monarch Street	K12
39	Monaville Avenue	C20
39	Monaville Close	C20
39	Monaville Drive	C21
39	Monaville Gardens	C21
39	Monaville Park	C20
19	Moneyrea Street	N12
7	Monkscoole House	M4
4	Monkstown Ave	M2
4	Monkstown Gdns	M1
4	Monkstown Road	M1
29	Montgomery Ct	P14
43	Montgomery Drive	E22
29	Montgomery Rd	P14
11	Montgomery St	M11
11	Montreal Street	J10
11	Montreal Street	J10
19	Montrose Street	N11
19	Montrose St Sth	N11
19	Montrose Walk	N11
27	Moonstone St	K14
25	Moor Park Ave	G15
25	Moor Park Drive	G15
25	Moor Park Gdns	G15
25	Moor Park Mews	G15
26	Mooreland Cres	H14
25	Mooreland Drive	H14
26	Mooreland Park	H14
17	Moore's Place	L12
19	Moorfield Street	P12
19	Moorgate Street	P12
38	Moorland Court	B20
38	Moorland Drive	B20
38	Moorland Park	B20
6	Moorland Avenue	K4
43	Morningside	E23
28	Mornington	M15
28	Mornington Mews	M15
28	Mornington Place	M15
17	Morpeth Street	K11
14	Morven Park	V12
14	Moscow Road	Q8
17	Moscow Street	K11
40	Moss Road	E19
3	Moss Road	J2
14	Moss Road	T9
3	Mossbank	K1
1	Mossgrove Park	J3
32	Mosside Mews	E18
32	Mosside Road	E18
17	Mossvale Street	J10
14	Motelands	R10
25	Mount Aboo Park	H16
16	Mount Alverno	G12
11	Mount Carmel	L8
18	Mount Charles	L13
8	Mount Coole Park	K7
11	Mount Eden Ct	J10
27	Mount Eden Park	K15
29	Mount Merrion Ave	N14
29	Mount Merrion Cres	N14
29	Mount Merrion Drive	N14
29	Mount Merrion Gdns	N14
29	Mount Merrion Park	N14
29	Mount Michael Drive	N15
29	Mount Michael Grove	N15
36	Mount Michael Pk	N16
29	Mount Michael View	N15
36	Mount Oriel	N16
28	Mount Pleasant	L14
5	Mount Pleasant Ave	N1
5	Mount Pleasant Drive	N1
5	Mount Pleasant Gdns	N1
5	Mount Pleasant Lane	N1
5	Mount Pleasant Park	N1
5	Mount Pleasant Road	N1
27	Mount Prospect Park	K13
43	Mount Royal	F22
19	Mount Street	M9
19	Mount Street	N12
18	Mount St South	N12
9	Mount Vernon Ct	L8
9	Mount Vernon Dr	L8
9	Mount Vernon Gdns	L8
9	Mount Vernon Grove	M8
9	Mount Vernon Lane	M8
9	Mount Vernon Park	L7
9	Mount Vernon Pass	M8
9	Mount Vernon Rd	M8
9	Mount Vernon Walk	M8
42	Mountain Vale Park	C21
10	Mountainhill Lane	H8
10	Mountainhill Road	H8
10	Mountainhill Walk	H8
3	Mountainvale Cr	J3
3	Mountainvale Dri	J3
3	Mountainvale Gds	J3
3	Mountainvale Rd	J3
10	Mountainview Dr	J10
10	Mountainview Gds	J10
10	Mountainview Parade	J10
10	Mountainview Pk	J10
10	Mountainview Pl	J10
17	Mountcashel St	J11
12	Mountcollyer Ave	L9
12	Mountcollyer Cl	L9
12	Mountcollyer Rd	M9
12	Mountcollyer St	L9
8	Mountcoole Gdns	K7
18	Mountforde Court	N11
	(Cuirt Chnocan Forde)	
18	Mountforde Drive	N11
	(Ceide Thulach Forde)	
18	Mountforde Gdns	N11
	(Garraithe Chnocn Ford)	
19	Mountforde Park	N11
19	Mountforde Road	N11
	(Bothar Thulach Forde)	
17	Mountjoy Street	K11
18	Mountpottinger Link	N11
	(Lub Thulach Phoitinser)	
19	Mountpottinger Road	N11
	(Bothar Thulach Phoitinseir)	
22	Mount-Regan Ave	U11
11	Mountview Court	K10
39	Mountview Drive	E19
39	Mountview Park	E19
7	Mountview Pass	N4
5	Mountview Place	N4
11	Mountview St	K10
19	Mourne Street	P11
38	Mourne View Crescent	B20
38	Mourne View Park	B20
4	Mournebeg Drive	M3
4	Mournebeg Way	M4
4	Movilla Park	M3
27	Mowhan Street	K14
28	Moyallen Gardens	M15
16	Moyard Crescent	H11
16	Moyard Park	H11
16	Moyard Parade	H11
35	Moyle Walk	L17
31	Moyne Park	S13
3	Moyola Park	J3
23	Moyra Cresent	V13
5	Mulberry Cres	M1
5	Mulberry Grange	M1
5	Mulberry Mews	M1
32	Mulberry Park	E17
5	Mulberry Park	M1
5	Mulderg Drive	L5
17	Mulhouse Road	K12
24	Mulroy Park	F14
17	Murray Street	L12
13	Musgrave Channel Rd	P9
26	Musgrave Park Ct	J15
25	Musgrave Manor	H14
18	Musgrave Street	M11
18	Music Hall Court	M11
18	Music Hall Lane	M11
44	My Lady's Mile	S7
19	My Lady's Road	N12
36	Myrtledene Drive	N17
36	Myrtledene Road	N17
27	Myrtlefiend Manor	J15
27	Myrtlefield Park	K15
17	**NANSEN STREET**	**J12**
17	Napier Street	L12
25	Naroon Park	F14
25	Navan Green	G14
9	Navarra Place	L5
20	Neill's Hill Park	Q12
17	Nelson Court	K11
17	Nelson Square	K11
12	Nelson Street	M10
4	Nendrum Gardens	M3
19	Nendrum Gardens	P12
32	Netherlands Dr	F16
32	Netherlands Park	F16
21	Netherleigh Park	S11
38	Nettlehill Road	B19
40	Nevis's Row	F19
19	Nevis Avenue	P11
16	New Barnsley Cres	G12
16	New Barnsley Dr	H12
16	New Barnsley Gds	H12
16	New Barnsley Green	H12
16	New Barnsley Grove	H12
16	New Barnsley Park	H12
16	New Barnsley Pde	H12
10	New Farm Lane	H8
27	New Forge Dale	K15
27	New Forge Grange	K15
35	New Forge Lane	K16
23	New Line	V13
12	New Lodge Place	L10
12	New Lodge Road	L10
43	New Street	E21
19	Newcastle Manor	N11
19	Newcastle Street	N11
11	Newington Ave	L9
11	Newington St	L9
11	Newport Court	K10
19	Newry Street	N12
7	Newton Gardens	M5
37	Newton Heights	P16
36	Newton Park	N16
19	Newtownards Rd	N11
36	Newtownbreda Ct	M16
36	Newtownbreda Road	M16
2	Nicholson Drive	H2
42	Nicholson Gardens	D22
17	Ninth Street	K11
19	Norbloom Gdns	P12
16	Norbury Street	H13
16	Norfolk Drive	H13
16	Norfolk Gardens	H13
25	Norfolk Grove	H13
16	Norfolk Parade	H13
16	Norfolk Road	H13
16	Norfolk Way	H13
16	Norglen Court	H12
16	Norglen Cresent	H13
16	Norglen Drive	H13
16	Norglen Gardens	H13
16	Norglen Grove	H12
16	Norglen Parade	G12
16	Norglen Parade	H12
16	Norglen Road	G13
22	Normandy Court	V11
29	North Bank	N14
17	North Boundary St	L11
8	North Circular Road	K7
42	North Circular Rd	D21
44	North Close	S7
30	North Derby St	M9
44	North Down	T5
	Coastal Path	
19	North Gardens	Q12

STREET INDEX

Page	Street	Grid Ref	Page	Street	Grid Ref	Page	Street	Grid Ref	Page	Street	Grid Ref
25	North Green	G14	22	Old Dundonald Rd	U12	25	Orchardville Cres	H15	12	Parkmount Close	L9
18	North Hill Street	L10	33	Old Golf Course Rd	F16	25	Orchardville Gdns	H15	2	Parkmount Court	F2
17	North Howard Ct	K11	15	Old Holywood Rd	S9	11	Oregon Gardens	J10	9	Parkmount Gdns	M7
17	Nth Howard Link	K11	14	Old Holywood Rd	R10		(Orkan Gairdens)		9	Parkmount Lane	M7
17	North Howard St	K11	14	Old Holywood Rd	R10	11	Orient Gardens	K9	9	Parkmount Parade	L7
17	North Howard Walk	K11	4	Old Irish Highway	M3	17	Orkney Street	K10	9	Parkmount Pass	M7
17	North King St	L11	11	Old Lodge Road	K10	34	Orlock Square	H16	9	Parkmount Place	M7
25	North Link	H14	5	Old Manse Court	P2	18	Ormeau Avenue	L12	2	Parkmount Road	F2
28	North Parade	M13	5	Old Manse Road	N2	28	Ormeau Embankment	M13	9	Parkmount Road	L7
12	North Queen St	M9	23	Old Mill Close	W12	28	Ormeau Road	M13	12	Parkmount Street	L9
20	North Road	Q12	2	Old Mill Crescent	F2	18	Ormeau Street	M12	9	Parkmount Tce	M7
21	North Sperrin	T12	23	Old Mill Dale	W12	20	Ormiston Cres	R11	9	Parkmount Way	M7
18	North Street	L11	7	Old Mill Drive	M5	20	Ormiston Drive	R11	11	Parkside Gardens	L9
18	North St Arcade	L11	23	Old Mill Grove	W12	20	Ormiston Gardens	R12	43	Parkview	E21
27	Northbrook Gdns	K13	23	Old Mill Heights	W12	20	Ormiston Parade	R11	11	*Parkview Court	K10
27	Northbrook St	K13	23	Old Mill Heights	W12	20	Ormiston Park	R11		(Glenview Street)	
30	Northern Road	M9	23	Old Mill Meadows	W12	3	Ormonde Avenue	H2	11	Parkville Court	L8
30	Northfield Rise	R13	23	Old Mill Mews	W12	33	Ormonde Avenue	G16	21	Parkvue Manor	S13
17	Northland Court	K11	23	Old Mill Park	W12	33	Ormonde Gardens	P13	14	Parkway	R10
17	Northland Street	K11	23	Old Mill Rise	W12	33	Ormonde Park	G16	39	Parkwood	E20
25	Northlands Park	H15	10	Old Mill Road	H8	33	Ormonde Park	G16	20	Pasadena Gardens	Q12
17	Northumberland St	K11	10	Old Mill Way	H8	33	Orpen Drive	H16	18	Patterson's Place	L11
11	Northwick Drive	J9	35	Old Milltown Road	L17	33	Orpen Road	H16	44	Patton's Lane	S6
12	Northwood Cres	M8	44	Old Quay Court	T6	33	Orpen Avenue	H16	12	Paulett Avenue	N12
12	Northwood Drive	M9	44	Old Quay Road	T6	33	Orpen Park	H16	44	Pavilions Office Park	S7
12	Northwood Pde	M8	37	Old Saintfield Rd	P18	23	Orsay Walk	W12	19	Paxton Street	N12
12	Northwood Road	L8	24	Old Suffolk Road	F14	3	Orwood Mews	K3	19	Pearl Court	N12
4	Norton Drive	K15	7	Old Throne Park	L5	27	Osborne Drive	K14	19	Pearl Street	N12
20	Norwood Avenue	Q11	11	Old Westland Rd	K8	27	Osborne Gardens	K14	20	Pembridge Court	R11
20	Norwood Crescent	Q10	34	Olde Forge Manor	H17	27	Osborne Park	K15	20	Pembridge Mews	Q12
20	Norwood Court	Q10	11	Oldpark Avenue	K9	27	Osborne Place	J14	24	Pembroke Court	E15
20	Norwood Drive	Q11	38	Oldpark Road	B19	17	Osman Street	K11	24	Pembroke Loop Road	E15
20	Norwood Gardens	R11	11	Oldpark Road	J8	3	Osterley Park	K3	24	Pembroke Manor	E15
20	Norwood Grove	Q11	11	Oldpark Square	K9	17	Oswald Park	L12	17	Pembroke Street	K12
44	Norwood Lane	S7	11	Oldpark Terrace	K9	11	Ottawa Street	K9	3	Pembrooke Court	J2
20	Norwood Park	R11	3	Oldwood	H2	19	Oval Street	P11	3	Pembrooke Mews	J2
17	Norwood Street	L12	27	Olive Street	J10	7	Owenreagh Close	M4	28	Penge Gardens	L14
27	Notting Hill	K14	27	Olympia Drive	K13	7	Owenreagh Drive	M4	36	Pennington Park	N16
27	Notting Hill Court	L14	27	Olympia Parade	K13	16	Owenvale Mews	H11	28	Penrose Street	M13
27	Notting Hill Manor	K14	27	Olympia Street	K13	25	Owenvarragh Gds	H14	18	*Pepperhill Street	L11
17	Nubia Street	K12	19	Omeath Street	N12	25	Owenvarragh Park	H14		(Plunkett Court)	
44	Nuns Walk	T7	4	O'Neill Road	L3	39	Oxford Avenue	D20	17	Percy Place	K11
			17	O'Neill Street	K11	18	Oxford Street	M11	17	Percy Street	K11
3	OAK FERN	H2	44	O'Neill's Place	S6				17	Percy Street	K11
18	Oak Street	L12	29	Onslow Gardens	N13	11	PACIFIC AVENUE	L9	17	Pernau Street	K11
18	Oak Way	L12	29	Onslow Parade	N13	18	Pakenham Mews	L12	17	Perry Court	N12
19	Oakdale Street	P11	29	Onslow Park	N13	18	Pakenham Street	L12	11	Peter's Hill	L11
19	Oakdene Drive	P11	11	Ophir Gardens	K8	15	Palace Gardens	L8	34	Phennick Drive	H16
19	Oakdene Parade	P11	38	Orange Hall Lane	B20	15	Palace Grove	S8	29	Picardy Avenue	P14
30	Oakhill	Q14	20	Orangefield Av	Q12	15	Palace Mews	S8	18	Pilot Place	M10
33	Oakhurst Avenue	G16	29	Orangefield Cres	P13	28	Palestine Street	M13	18	Pilot Street	M10
19	Oakland Avenue	Q11	20	Orangefield Drive	Q12	39	Palmer Avenue	D20	11	Pim Street	L10
33	Oakland Way	F18	20	Orangefield		11	Palmer Court	J10	17	Pim's Avenue	P11
18	Oakleigh Park	N13		Drive South		11	Palmer Street	J10	33	Pine Cross	F18
44	Oakley Avenue	S7	19	Orangefield Gdns	Q12	20	Palmerston Park	Q10	44	Pine Grove	S8
10	Oakley Street	H9	19	Orangefield Green	Q12	20	Palmerston Road	Q10	18	Pine Street	M12
17	Oakman Street	J12	19	Orangefield Grove	Q12	19	Pandora Street	K12	18	Pine Way	M12
12	Oakmount Drive	M9	19	Orangefield Lane	Q12	19	Pansy Street	N11	39	Pinecroft Park	C20
39	Oakridge Avenue	D19	19	Orangefield Pde	Q12	24	Pantridge Road	E15	6	Pineview Drive	L5
39	Oakridge Crescent	D19	19	Orangefield Park	Q12	17	Paris Street	K10	6	Pineview Gardens	L5
39	Oakridge Gardens	D19	20	Orangefield Road	Q12	22	Park Avenue	U12	6	Pineview Park	L5
39	Oakridge Park	D19	25	Oranmore Drive	F15	19	Park Avenue	P11	6	Pineview Road	L5
33	Oakvale Court	F16	17	Oranmore Street	J11	44	Park Avenue	S7	35	Piney Hills	K16
33	Oakvale Gardens	F16	29	Orby Court	P12	22	Park Drive	U12	35	Piney Lane	K16
5	Oakwood	N3	30	Orby Close	Q13	44	Park Drive	S7	35	Piney Park	K16
27	Oakwood Court	K15	30	Orby Drive	Q13	19	Park Grange	P11	35	Piney Walk	K16
27	Oakwood Grove	K15	19	Orby Gardens	P12	27	Park Lane	L13	35	Piney Way	K16
27	Oakwood Mews	K15	19	Orby Grange	P12	36	Park Lodge	M16	22	Pinkerton Walk	L10
27	Oakwood Park	L9	19	Orby Green	P13	2	Park Manor	F2	22	Pipers Field	U12
29	Oberon Street	N13	19	Orby Grove	P13	33	Park Mews	F16	29	Pirrie Park Gdns	N13
17	Oceanic Avenue	L9	19	Orby Link	P12	43	Park Parade	E21	20	Pirrie Road	R11
12	O'Dempsey St	M9	19	Orby Mews	P12	18	Park Parade	N12	19	Pitt Place	N11
17	Odessa Street	K11	19	Orby Parade	P13	2	Park Road	F2	29	Pittsburg Street	M9
	(Sraid Odasa)		19	Orby Park	P12	28	Park Road	M13	43	Plantation Ave	F22
19	Ogilvie Street	N12	19	Orby Path	P13	26	Park Royal Balmoral	J15	3	Plantation Avenue	K1
17	Ohio Street	J10	29	Orby Place	P13	12	Parkend Street	L9	43	Plantation Close	E22
8	Old Cavehill Road	K7	19	Orby Road	P12	19	Parker Street	P11	43	Plantation Drive	E22
25	Old Channel Road	N11	30	Orby Street	Q13	19	Parkgate Avenue	P11	43	Plantation Grove	F22
7	Old Church Road	M5	42	Orchard Close	D22	19	Parkgate Crescent	P11	43	Plantation Mews	F22
34	Old Coach Ave	J17	21	Orchard Close	S13	19	Parkgate Drive	P11	43	Plantation Road	F22
34	Old Coach Gdns	J17	14	Orchard Court	R9	19	Parkgate Gardens	P11	3	Plantation Way	K1
34	Old Coach Rd	J17	14	Orchard Court	R9	19	Parkgate Parade	P11	44	Plas Merdyn	T7
24	Old Colin	E15	14	Orchard Lane	R10	44	Parkhouse Manor	T6	17	Plevna Park	K11
24	Old Colin Road	D16	36	Orchard Rise	N16	44	Parkland Avenue	C20	17	Plunkett Court	L11
44	Old Cultra Lane	T5	12	Orchard Street	M10	39	Parkland Drive	C20		(Cuirt Phluinceid)	
44	Old Cultra Road	T5	29	Orchard Vale	P14	28	Parkmore Street	M14	17	Pollard Close	J11
			25	Orchardville Ave	H15	40	Parkmount	E21		(Clos Pholaird)	

STREET INDEX

Page		Grid Ref	Page		Grid Ref	Page		Grid Ref	Page		Grid Ref
17	Pollard Street	**J11**	40	Queensway	**E20**	29	Ravensdene Park Gdns	**N13**	39	Riverside Drive	**E20**
	(Sraid Pholaird)		32	Queensway Park	**E18**	30	Ravenswood Cres	**R13**	24	Riverside Mews	**F15**
12	Pollock Road	**M10**	19	Quinton Street	**P12**	30	Ravenswood Park	**R13**	17	*Riverside Square	**K12**
29	Pommern Parade	**P13**	44	Quinville	**T7**	42	Ravernet Road	**D23**		(Blackwater Way)	
19	Pomona Avenue	**P11**				22	Reaville Park	**U12**	42	Riverside Terrace	**D22**
39	Pond Park Avenue	**C20**	28	**RABY STREET**	**M14**	44	Redburn Square	**S6**	17	Riverside Way	**K12**
39	Pond Park Crescent	**C20**	19	Radnor Street	**N12**	19	Redcar Street	**N12**	28	Riverview Street	**L14**
38	Pond Park Road	**B19**	5	Raholp Park	**N2**	19	Redcliffe Drive	**P11**	23	Robb's Court	**V12**
11	Ponsonby Ave	**L9**	40	Railway Cottages	**E19**	19	Redcliffe Parade	**P11**	23	Robb's Road	**V12**
19	Portallo Street	**N12**	5	Railway Court	**N1**	19	Redcliffe Street	**P11**	12	Robina Court	**L9**
33	Porter Park	**H16**	33	Railway Street	**G17**	34	Redhill Manor	**H16**	12	Robina Street	**L9**
3	Portland Avenue	**J3**	17	Railway Street	**L12**	39	Redpoll Avenue	**C20**	29	Rochester Ave	**P14**
18	Portland Place	**L10**	32	Railway Street	**F18**	5	Redwood	**N2**	30	Rochester Court	**Q14**
25	Portnamona Ct	**G13**	42	Railway Street	**D21**	32	Redwood Court	**F18**	29	Rochester Drive	**P14**
7	*Portrosse Park	**M4**	32	Railway View	**F18**	32	Redwood Dale	**F18**	29	Rochester Park	**P14**
	(Owenreagh Drive)		18	Rainey Way	**L12**	32	Redwood Grove	**F18**	29	Rochester Road	**P14**
39	Portulla Drive	**C20**	17	Raleigh Street	**K10**	32	Redwood Mews	**F18**	18	Rochester Street	**L12**
7	Portulla Park	**M4**	25	Ramoan Drive	**G14**	23	Regent Court	**W11**	16	Rock Grove	**H12**
18	Posnett Court	**L12**	25	Ramoan Drive	**G14**	17	Regent Street	**L10**	17	Rockdale Street	**J12**
18	Posnett Street	**L12**	25	Ramoan Gardens	**G14**	29	Reid Street	**N13**	17	Rockland Street	**K12**
19	Pottinger Street	**N12**	25	Ramoan Gardens	**G14**	4	Renagh Park	**N3**	22	Rockmore Road	**J12**
18	Pottinger's Court	**M11**	34	Ramore Park	**J16**	17	Renfrew Walk	**L12**	22	Rockmount	**U12**
18	Pottinger's Entry	**M11**	27	Randal Park	**K14**	17	Renwick Street	**L12**	16	Rockmount St	**J12**
18	Powerscourt Pl	**M13**	20	Ranelagh Street	**N13**	19	Riada Close	**N11**	4	Rockview Lane	**K3**
18	Powerscourt St	**M13**	20	Ranfurly Drive	**Q11**	19	Ribble Street	**P11**	17	Rockview Street	**K13**
12	Premier Drive	**L8**	23	Rank Road	**V12**	19	Richardson Street	**N12**	14	Rockville Court	**Q10**
12	Premier Grove	**L8**	18	Raphael Street	**M12**	44	Richdale Drive	**T6**	14	Rockville Mews	**Q10**
11	Prestwick Drive	**J8**	19	Ratcliffe Street	**N11**	20	Richhill Crescent	**R12**	17	Rockville Street	**J12**
11	Prestwick Park	**J8**	18	*Rathbone Street	**M12**	20	Richhill Park	**R12**	29	Rocky Road	**P15**
28	Pretoria Street	**L13**		(Little May Street)		39	Richmond Ave	**C20**	31	Rocky Road	**S14**
41	Priests Lane	**C23**	27	Rathcool Street	**K14**	14	Richmond Ave	**R9**	30	Roddens Cres	**Q13**
42	Primrose Garden Village	**D22**	7	Rathcoole Close	**M5**	3	Richmond Avenue	**J2**	30	Roddens Gardens	**Q13**
37	Primrose Hill	**N17**	7	Rathcoole Drive	**M4**	14	Richmond Close	**R9**	30	Roddens Park	**Q13**
28	Primrose Street	**M14**	7	Rathcoole Gdns	**M5**	40	Richmond Court	**E20**	17	Roden Pass	**K12**
10	Primrose Street	**H9**	7	Rathdrum Park	**M4**	14	Richmond Court	**R9**	17	Roden Square	**K12**
17	Prince Andrew Gdns	**K12**	27	Rathdrum Street	**K14**	39	Richmond Crescent	**C20**	17	Roden Street	**K12**
17	Prince Andrew Pk	**K12**	4	Rathfern Way	**M3**	3	Richmond Crescent	**J2**	17	Roden Street	**K12**
3	Prince Charles Way	**K3**	27	Rathgar Street	**K14**	39	Richmond Drive	**C20**	17	Roden Way	**K12**
28	Prince Edward Drive	**L14**	25	Rath Mor	**G15**	3	Richmond Drive	**J2**	17	Rodney Drive	**J13**
28	Prince Edward Gdns	**L14**	11	Rathlin Street	**J10**	3	Richmond Gdns	**J2**	17	Rodney Parade	**J13**
28	Prince Edward Park	**L14**	33	Rathmore Avenue	**H16**	14	Richmond Green	**R9**	2	Rogan Manor	**G2**
21	Prince Of Wales Ave	**S11**	42	Rathmore Avenue	**C21**	3	Richmond Grove	**J2**	36	Rogers Park	**N16**
30	Prince Regent Rd	**Q13**	7	Rathmore Drive	**M4**	14	Richmond Hts	**R9**	36	Rogers Place	**N16**
42	Prince William Road	**C21**	33	Rathmore Gdns	**H16**	26	Richmond Mews	**H15**	17	Roosevelt Rise	**K12**
5	Prince's Avenue	**M3**	42	Rathmore Park	**C21**	39	Richmond Mews	**C20**	17	Roosevelt Square	**K12**
5	Prince's Crescent	**M3**	33	Rathmore Park	**H16**	3	Richmond Parade	**J2**	17	Roosevelt Street	**K12**
18	Prince's Dock St	**M10**	18	Rathmore Street	**N12**	3	Richmond Park	**J2**	11	Rosapenna Court	**K10**
5	Prince's Drive	**M3**	7	Rathmore Way	**L4**	26	Richmond Park	**H15**	11	Rosapenna Drive	**K9**
5	Prince's Park	**M3**	7	Rathmullan Drive	**M4**	27	Richmond Park	**L14**	11	Rosapenna Parade	**K9**
15	Prior's Lea	**S8**	38	Rathvarna Avenue	**B20**	39	Richmond Park	**C20**	24	Rosapenna Sq	**F14**
40	Priory Close	**E19**	38	Rathvarna Close	**B20**	3	Richmond Pk East	**J2**	11	Rosapenna Street	**K10**
44	Priory End	**S7**	38	Rathvarna Drive	**B20**	3	Richmond Road	**J2**	11	Rosapenna Walk	**K9**
26	Priory Gardens	**H15**	38	Rathvarna Gardens	**B20**	11	Richmond Square	**L9**	4	Roscor Square	**M4**
15	Priory Park	**J15**	38	Rathvarna Park	**B20**	3	Richmond Way	**J2**	3	Rose Drive	**J3**
44	Priory Park	**T6**	38	Rathvarna Walk	**B20**	17	Richview Street	**K12**	39	Rose Park	**D19**
40	Priory Terrace	**E19**	42	Ravarnet Walk	**C22**	42	Ridgeway Street	**D21**	3	Rose Park	**J3**
22	Private Avenue	**U12**	4	Ravelston Ave	**K1**	28	Ridgeway Street	**L14**	11	Rosebank Court	**K10**
42	Prospect Crescent	**D21**	4	Ravelston Cres	**K1**	17	Riga Street	**K11**	11	Rosebank Street	**J10**
42	Prospect Mews	**D21**	4	Ravelston Drive	**K2**	11	Rigby Close	**K8**	19	Rosebery Gdns	**N12**
39	Prospect Park	**C20**	4	Ravelston Gdns	**K1**	25	Ringford Cres	**F15**	19	Rosebery Road	**N12**
42	Prospect Terrace	**S6**	3	Ravelston Grove	**K1**	25	Ringford Park	**F15**	19	Rosebery Street	**P12**
28	Purdys Lane	**N15**	4	Ravelston Link	**K1**	25	Rinnalea Close	**F14**	27	Roseland Place	**L12**
35	Purdysburn Hill	**L18**	4	Ravelston Park	**K1**	24	Rinnalea Gardens	**F14**	11	Roseleigh Street	**K9**
36	Purdysburn Road	**M17**	4	Ravelston Parade	**K2**	25	Rinnalea Grove	**F14**	42	Rosemary Drive	**D22**
			4	Ravelston Road	**K1**	25	Rinnalea Walk	**F14**	27	Rosemary Park	**K16**
17	**QUADRANT PLACE**	**L11**	4	Ravelston Way	**F14**	24	Rinnalea Way	**F14**	18	Rosemary Street	**L11**
30	Quarry Cottages	**U12**	19	Ravenhill Avenue	**N13**	12	Ritchie Street	**M9**	41	Rosemeadows	**B21**
22	Quarry Hill	**R14**	19	Ravenhill Court	**N13**	25	River Close	**G15**	21	Rosemount Ave	**T12**
22	Quarry Lane	**U12**	18	Ravenhill Cres	**N12**	32	River Court	**F18**	5	Rosemount Cres	**N1**
15	Quarry Road	**S10**	28	Ravenhill Gardens	**N13**	32	River Grove	**F18**	11	Rosemount Gdns	**L9**
7	Quay Road	**M5**	19	Ravenhill Mews	**N12**	32	River Mews	**F18**	5	Rosemount Park	**N1**
18	Queen Street	**L11**	19	Ravenhill Parade	**N13**	40	River Road	**F19**	30	Rosemount Park	**Q14**
12	Queen Victoria Gdns	**L8**	19	Ravenhill Park	**N13**	32	River Road	**F18**	21	Rosepark	**T12**
19	Queen Victoria St	**P11**	29	Ravenhill Park Gds	**N14**	18	River Terrace	**M12**	21	Rosepark East	**T12**
18	Queen's Arcade	**L11**	19	Ravenhill Reach	**M12**	5	River Walk	**M1**	21	Rosepark Central	**T12**
3	Queens Avenue	**J2**	19	Ravenhill Reach Ct	**M12**	33	Riverbank	**G18**	21	Rosepark Meadows	**T12**
3	Queens Crescent	**J2**	19	Ravenhill Reach Mws	**M12**	25	Riverdale Close	**H14**	21	Rosepark South	**T12**
3	Queens Drive	**J2**	28	Ravenhill Road	**N13**	25	Riverdale Gardens	**H14**	21	Rosepark West	**T12**
3	Queens Gardens	**J2**	18	Ravenhill Street	**N12**	25	Riverdale Pk Ave	**G14**	28	Rosetta Avenue	**M14**
3	Queens Park	**J3**	19	Ravenscroft Ave	**P11**	25	Riverdale Pk Dr	**G14**	14	Rosetta Court	**M14**
12	Queen's Parade	**L10**	19	Ravenscroft St	**P11**	25	Riverdale Pk East	**H14**	14	Rosetta Drive	**M14**
28	Queen's Quay	**M11**	19	Ravensdale	**K1**	25	Riverdale Pk Nth	**G14**	28	Rosetta Parade	**M14**
29	Queen's Road	**N10**	19	Ravensdale Cres	**N12**	25	Riverdale Pk Sth	**H15**	28	Rosetta Park	**N14**
43	Queen's Road	**E21**	19	Ravensdale St	**N12**	25	Riverdale Pk West	**G14**	14	Rosetta Park	**N14**
11	Queen's Square	**M11**	29	Ravensdene Cres	**N13**	25	Riverdale Place	**H14**	29	Rosetta Road	**N14**
29	Queensberry Park	**N14**	29	Ravensdene Mws	**N13**	42	Rivergate Lane	**C23**	29	Rosetta Rd East	**N14**
11	Queensland St	**K10**	28	Ravensdene Park	**N13**	53	Riverside	**F18**	28	Rosetta Way	**N14**
32	Queensway	**E18**									

STREET INDEX

Page	Street	Grid Ref
41	Rosevale Meadows	B22
11	Rosevale Street	K10
43	Roseville Gardens	E21
43	Roseville Park	E21
43	Roseville Walk	E21
38	Rosewood	B20
11	Rosewood Court	K10
38	Rosewood Glen	B20
30	Rosewood Park	Q14
11	Rosewood Street	K10
25	Rosgoill Drive	F14
25	Rosgoill Gardens	F14
25	Rosgoill Park	G14
21	Roslin Gardens	T12
19	Roslyn Street	N12
23	Rosneath Court	W12
23	Rosneath Gardens	W12
17	Ross Court	K11
17	Ross Rise	K11
17	Ross Road	K11
17	Ross Street	K11
8	Rosscoole Park	J7
37	Rossdale Gardens	P17
37	Rossdale Glen	P17
37	Rossdale Heights	P17
37	Rossdale Park	P16
37	Rossdale Road	P17
7	Rosslea Way	M4
42	Rosslyn Park	C21
28	Rossmore Ave	M14
28	Rossmore Cres	M14
28	Rossmore Drive	M14
28	Rossmore Park	M14
25	Rossnareen Ave	G14
25	Rossnareen Court	G14
25	Rossnareen Park	G14
25	Rossnareen Road	G14
5	Rosstulla Avenue	P2
5	Rosstulla Drive	P2
5	Rosstulla Park	P2
33	Rothsay Square	K10
18	Rotterdam Court	M11
18	Rotterdam Street	M11
23	Roumania Rise	K11
19	Roundhill Street	N11
3	Rowan Court	K2
33	Rowan Drive	F18
3	Rowan Grove	K1
17	Rowland Way	L12
18	Royal Avenue	L11
36	Royal Lodge Ave	N17
36	Royal Lodge Ct	N17
36	Royal Lodge Gdns	N17
36	Royal Lodge Mews	N17
36	Royal Lodge Park	N17
36	Royal Lodge Road	M17
36	Royal Lodge Road	N17
33	Royal Mews	G17
5	Royal Oaks	N1
36	Royal Oaks	N17
28	Rugby Avenue	M13
28	Rugby Court	M13
28	Rugby Mews	L13
28	Rugby Parade	L13
28	Rugby Road	L13
28	Rugby Street	L13
17	Rumford Street	K11
27	Runnymede Drive	K13
27	Runnymede Pde	K13
3	Rural Gardens	J3
1	Rusheen Gardens	M4
28	Rushfield Avenue	M14
41	Rushmore Crescent	B21
41	Rushmore Drive	B21
41	Rushmore Gardens	B21
41	Rushmore Grove	B21
41	Rushmore Park	B21
17	Rusholme Street	K10
42	Ruskin Heights	D23
31	Ruskin Park	D23
31	Russell Park	T13
17	Russell Place	M12
18	Russell Street	M12
31	Rutherglen St	J10
28	Rutland Street	M13
30	Ryan Park	R15
43	Ryans Court	E22
17	Rydalmere Street	K12
17	**SACKVILLE COURT**	**L11**
42	Sackville Street	D21
19	Sagimor Gardens	P12
43	Saintfield Mews	E22
43	Saintfield Park	E21
43	Saintfield Road	E22
36	Saintfield Road	N16
42	Saintsbury Avenue	D23
44	Saleen Park	T6
11	Salisbury Avenue	K8
18	Salisbury Court	L12
11	Salisbury Gardens	K8
18	Salisbury Lane	L12
33	Salisbury Place	G17
18	Salisbury Street	L12
24	Sally Garden Lane	E15
3	Sally Gardens	J3
3	Sally Gardens	J3
17	Samuel Street	L11
17	Sancroft Street	K10
7	Sanda Road	M5
19	Sandbrook Gdns	P10
19	Sandbrook Grove	P10
19	Sandbrook Park	P10
19	Sandford Avenue	Q12
20	Sandhill Drive	Q12
20	Sandhill Gardens	Q12
20	Sandhill Green	Q12
20	Sandhill Parade	Q12
20	Sandhill Park	Q12
28	Sandhurst Drive	L13
28	Sandhurst Gdns	L13
18	Sandhurst Road	M13
20	Sandown Drive	Q12
42	Sandown Park	C21
20	Sandown Park	R12
20	Sandown Pk 5th	Q12
20	Sandown Road	Q12
30	Sandringham Mews	R12
27	Sandringham St	K13
40	Sandy Lane	F20
17	Sandy Row	L12
3	Sandyholme Park	H3
2	Sandyholme Way	H3
3	Sandyknowes Av	H3
3	Sandyknowes Cr	H3
3	Sandyknowes Dr	H3
3	Sandyknowes Gds	H3
3	Sandyknowes Gro	H3
3	Sandyknowes Pk	H3
3	Sandyknowes Way	H3
27	Sandymount St	L14
42	Sans Souci Gardens	D21
27	Sans Souci Park	L14
11	Sarajac Crescent	K8
19	Sark Street	N11
19	*Saunders Close	N11
	(Scotch Row)	
11	Saunderson's Ct	K8
25	Sawel Hill	G14
42	Sawel Place	C21
20	Schomberg Ave	R11
17	Schomberg Drive	L12
20	Schomberg Lodge	R11
20	Schomberg Park	R11
17	Schomberg St	L12
14	School Court	R9
36	School Road	N16
31	School Road	S15
19	Scotch Row	N11
17	Scott Street	L12
19	Scotts Court	P11
18	Scrabo Street	M11
2	Scullions Road	H3
28	Seabank Parade	M8
12	Seabourne Parade	L8
19	Seaforde Court	N11
	(Cuirt Shui Forde)	
19	Seaforde Gardens	N11
19	Seaforde Street	N11
	(Straid Sut Forde)	
5	Seagoe Gardens	N2
12	Seagrove Parade	M8
12	Seagrove Place	L8
12	Seaholm Parade	L8
13	Seal Road	N8
12	Sealands Parade	L8
12	Seamount	M8
12	Seamount Parade	L8
33	Seamour Hill Vws	F17
44	Seapark Avenue	T6
44	Seapark Court	T6
12	Seapark Drive	L8
44	Seapark Grove	T6
44	Seapark Mews	T6
44	Seapark Road	T6
44	Seapark Terrace	T6
12	Seascape Parade	L8
12	Seaview Close	M8
12	Seaview Drive	M8
12	Seaview Drive	L8
12	Seaview Gardens	M8
3	Seaview Lane	J3
12	Seaview Street	M9
44	Seaview Terrace	S6
19	Sefton Drive	Q11
19	Sefton Park	Q11
17	Selby Court	K12
17	Selby Walk	K12
3	Sentry Hill Drive	J1
2	Sentry Lane	G2
42	Sepon Park	D21
5	Sequoia Heights	N2
40	Sequoia Park	E19
5	Serpentine Gdns	L5
7	Serpentine Pde	L6
7	Serpentine Road	L6
17	Servia Street	K12
18	Sevastopol St	K11
	(Sraid Seibheastopol)	
19	Severn Street	P11
18	Seymour Lane	M11
43	Seymour Park	E22
18	Seymour Row	M11
43	Seymour Street	E21
18	Seymour Street	M11
18	Shaftesbury Ave	M12
18	Shaftesbury Sq	L12
30	Shalom Park	Q14
18	Shamrock Court	N12
18	Shamrock Place	N12
18	Shamrock Street	N12
8	Shancoole Park	K7
11	Shandarragh Park	K8
39	Shandon	C20
30	Shandon Heights	R14
20	Shandon Park	R13
8	Shaneen Park	K7
8	Shangarry Park	K7
17	Shankill Parade	L11
17	Shankill Road	K11
17	Shankill Terrace	L11
8	Shanlieve Park	K7
25	Shanlieve Road	H14
11	Shannon Court	K10
11	Shannon Street	K10
28	Sharman Close	L15
28	Sharman Drive	L15
28	Sharman Gardens	L15
28	Sharman Park	L15
28	Sharman Road	L15
28	Sharman Way	L15
4	Sharonmore Ave	K2
4	Sharonmore Gdns	K2
4	Sharonmore Grn	L2
4	Sharonmore Pde	K2
4	Sharonmore Park	K2
39	Sharry Drive	D19
19	Shaw Street	P11
25	Shaw's Avenue	G14
25	Shaw's Close	F14
25	Shaw's Court	G14
25	Shaw's Park	G14
25	Shaw's Place	G14
25	Shaw's Road	G14
29	Shelbourne Road	N13
17	Sherbrook Close	L11
17	Sherbrook Tce	L10
11	Sheridan Court	L10
39	Sheridan Park	C19
11	Sheridan Street	L10
5	Sheringhurst Ct	M7
9	Sheringhurst Park	M7
3	Sherwood Ave	H2
3	Sherwood Parks	H2
29	Sheskin Way	N14
17	Shiels Street	J12
29	Shimna Close	N14
12	Ship Street	M10
18	Shipbuoy Street	M10
9	Shore Crescent	M7
7	Shore Road	M5
5	Shore Road	N3
5	Shore Road	P2
9	Shore Road	M7
44	Shore Rd	S6
12	Short Street	M10
18	Short Strand	M11
27	Shrewsbury Drive	J15
27	Shrewsbury Gdns	J15
27	Shrewsbury Park	K15
26	Sicily Park	H15
10	Silver Birch Courts	K11
10	Silverstream Ave	J8
10	Silverstream Cres	J8
10	Silverstream Dr	J8
10	Silverstream Gdns	J8
10	Silverstream Pde	J8
10	Silverstream Park	J8
	(Sillerburn Park)	
10	Silverstream Rd	H8
5	Silverstream Rd	P1
10	Silverstream Tce	H8
17	Silvio Street	K10
12	Sinclair Road	N9
20	Sinclair Street	Q12
19	Sintonville Ave	P11
39	Siskin Drive	C20
25	*Siulnamona Court	G13
	(Altnamona Court)	
12	Skegoneill Ave	L9
12	Skegoneill Drive	L9
12	Skegoneill Street	M8
18	Skipper Street	M11
19	Skipton Street	P11
39	Skyline Court	E20
39	Skyline Drive	E20
39	Skyline Gardens	E19
25	Slemish Way	H14
42	Slemish Way	C21
25	Sliabh Mor Heights	H13
25	Slieveban Drive	G14
8	Slievecoole Park	K7
8	Slievedarragh Pk	K7
25	Slievegallion Dr	G14
7	Slievegoland Park	L6
9	Slievemoyne Park	L7
8	Slievetoye Park	K7
27	Sloan Court	K13
43	Sloan Street	E21
11	Smithfield Sq Nth	L11
42	Smithfield Street	D21
7	Snakey Path	L5
11	Snugville Street	K10
17	Snugville Street	K11
19	Solway Street	N11
10	Somerdale Gdns	J9
10	Somerdale Park	J9
10	Somerdale Park	J9
28	Somerset Street	M14
11	Somerton Close	L8
11	Somerton Court	L8
11	Somerton Drive	L8
12	Somerton Gdns	L8
9	Somerton Grange	L7
11	Somerton Mews	L8
11	Somerton Park	L8
11	Somerton Road	L8
29	Somme Drive	P14
17	Sorella Street	K12
32	Soudan Street	K13
29	South Bank	N14
44	South Close	S7
35	South Crescent	L17
25	South Green	G14
10	South Link	H8
28	South Parade	M13
21	South Sperrin	T12
30	Southland Dale	R13

STREET INDEX

Page		Grid Ref	Page		Grid Ref	Page		Grid Ref	Page		Grid Ref
11	Southport Court	K10	22	St John's Wood Park	U11	18	Strand Walk	N11	3	Swanston Drive	J3
28	*Southview Cotts	M13	18	St Jude's Avenue	M14	19	Strandburn Court	P11	3	Swanston Gdns	H3
	(Southview Street)		28	St Jude's Cres	M14	19	Strandburn Cres	Q11	3	Swanston Park	H3
28	Southview Street	M13	28	St Jude's Parade	M14	19	Strandburn Drive	Q11	3	Swanston Road	H3
18	Southwell Street	L10	28	St Jude's Square	M14	19	Strandburn Gdns	P11	3	Swanston Rd Nth	H3
11	Spamount Street	L12	17	St Katharine Road	J13	19	Strandburn Pde	Q10	18	Swift Place	N12
44	Spencer Street	S7	18	St Kilda Court	M12	19	Strandburn Park	Q11	18	Swift Street	N12
21	Sperrin Drive	T12	18	St Kilda Street	M12	19	Strandburn St	P11	5	Sycamore Close	N1
21	Sperrin Park	T12	19	St Leonard's Cres	N11	28	Strandview St	L14	5	Sycamore Drive	N1
17	Spier's Place	K11	19	St Leonard's St	N11	27	Strangford Ave	J15	20	Sycamore Grove	Q11
5	Spinner Square	K11	17	*St Luke's Close	K11	39	Strangford Road	E20	5	Sycamore Park	N1
10	Spinnershill Lane	H8		(Morpeth Street)		28	Stranmillis Court	L14	28	Sydenham Ave	Q11
19	Spring Place	N12	17	St Luke's Walk	K11	28	Stranmillis Embankment	M13	19	Sydenham By-Pass	P10
19	Spring Street	N12	38	St Marks Wood	B20	28	Stranmillis Gdns	L13	28	Sydenham Cres	Q11
24	Springbank Close	E15	11	St Mary's Court	K10	28	Stranmillis Mews	L13	28	Sydenham Drive	Q11
24	Springbank Drive	E15	19	St Matthew's Ct	N11	28	Stranmillis Park	L13	18	Sydenham Flyover	N11
42	Springburn Park	D23		(Cuirt Naoimh Maitiu)		28	Stranmillis Reach	M13	19	Sydenham Gdns	Q11
16	Springdale Gdns	J11	25	St Meryl Park	H13	28	Stranmillis Road	L14	28	Sydenham Park	Q11
17	Springfield Ave	J11	19	St Patrick's Walk	N11	28	Stranmillis Street	L14	18	Sydenham Road	N11
	(Ascaill Chluanai)		42	St Paul's Court	C21	11	Stratford Gardens	J9	5	Sydney St West	K10
16	Springfield Close	H11	12	St Paul's Street	M10	34	Strathallen Park	H17	11	Sylvan Street	K9
17	Springfield Cres	J11	17	St Peter's Close	K11	44	Stratharm Court	S7	11	Symons Street	K12
	(Corran Chluanai)		17	St Peter's Place	K11	20	Strathearn Mews	Q11	11	Syringa Street	L10
17	Springfield Court	J11	17	St Peter's Sq East	K11	14	Stratheam Park	R10			
17	Springfield Drive	J11	17	St Peter's Sq N	K11	43	Strathearne Place	E21			
	(Ceide Chluanai)		3	St Quentin Ave	K3	11	Strathedin St	L10	18	TALBOT STREET	L11
16	Springfield Hts	H11	3	St Quentin Park	J3	9	Strathmore Park	L7	19	Tamar Street	P11
16	Springfield Meadows	J11	17	*St Stephen's Ct	L11	9	Strathmore Pk Nth	L7	19	Tamery Pass	N12
16	Springfield Park	H11		(Gardiner Place)		8	Strathmore Pk Sth	K7	44	Tarawood	T5
16	Springfield Parade	J11	12	St Vincent St	M8	11	Strathroy Park	J9	28	Tarawood Mews	M15
16	Springfield Road	J11	2	Stafford Road	G3	34	Strathyre Park	H17	25	Tardree Park	H14
	(Bóthar Chluanai)		18	Stanfield Place	M12	23	Strone Hill Court	W12	42	Tardree Place	C21
18	Springhill Avenue	H12	18	Stanfield Row	M12	23	Strone Hill Lane	W12	14	Tasmania Street	K10
16	Springhill Close	H12	17	Stanhope Drive	L11	23	Strone Park	W12	17	Tate's Avenue	K13
16	Springhill Crescent	H12	17	Stanhope Street	L12	17	Stroud Street	L12	27	Tate's Mews	K13
38	Springhill Crescent	B19	17	Stanley Court	L11	17	Sturgeon Street	L12	9	Taunton Avenue	L7
16	Springhill Drive	H12	17	Stanley Street	L12	19	Suffolk Avenue	F15	17	Tavanagh Street	K13
16	Springhill Gardens	H12	43	Stannus Place	E21	24	Suffolk Close	E14	42	Taylor Square	C22
16	Springhill Heights	H12	14	Station Mews	Q10	25	Suffolk Court	E14	17	Taylor Street	L12
38	Springhill Mews	B19	40	Station Road	E19	25	Suffolk Crescent	G15	10	Tedburn Park	H9
16	Springhill Rise	H12	5	Station Road	N3	25	Suffolk Drive	F15	18	Telfair Street	M11
16	Springmadden Ct	H12	5	Station Road	N3	24	Suffolk Heights	E14	32	Teeling Avenue	D16
16	Springmartin Rd	H11	14	Station Road	Q10	25	Suffolk Parade	G15	32	Teeling Grove	D16
10	Springvale Drive	H8	44	Station Road	T6	24	Suffolk Rise	E14	32	Teeling View	D16
10	Springvale Gdns	H8	18	Station Street	M11	24	Suffolk Road	F14	43	Templar Avenue	E22
10	Springvale Parade	H8	18	Station St Flyover	M11	24	Suffolk Way	E14	19	Temple Street	N12
10	Springvale Park	H8	33	Station View	G17	17	Sugarfield Street	K11	5	Templefinn Park	N2
5	Springview St	K12	18	Steam Mill Lane	M11	44	Sullivan Close	S6	19	Templemore Ave	N11
17	Springway Walk	K12	18	Stephen Street	L11	44	Sullivan Place	S6	19	Templemore Cl	N12
24	Spruce Hill	E14	18	Stewart Street	M12	17	Sultan Square	K11	19	Templemore Pl	N12
43	Spruce Street	E21	44	Stewart's Place	S6	11	Sultan Way	K11	19	Templemore St	N12
42	Sprucefield Court	D23	25	Stewartstown Ave	F14	11	Summer Street	K10	19	Tennent Street	K10
10	Squire's Hill Cres	H8	25	Stewartstown Gds	F14	21	Summerhill Ave	S12	11	Tern Street	N11
10	Squire's Hill Park	H8	25	Stewartstown Pk	F14	32	Summerhill Court	K10	17	Teutonic Gardens	L12
10	Squire's Hill Road	H8	32	Stewartstown Rd	E16	32	Summerhill Drive	F17	17	Thalia Street	K12
25	St Agnes Drive	H14	29	Stirling Avenue	P14	32	Summerhill Gdns	F17	17	Thames Court	J12
25	St Agnes Place	G14	29	Stirling Gardens	P14	32	Summerhill Grange	F17	17	Thames Street	J12
27	St Albans Gdns	L14	29	Stirling Road	P14	32	Summerhill Mews	F16	36	The Beeches	M17
17	St Andrew's Sq East	L12	39	Stockdam Glen	C20	32	Summerhill Park	F17	4	The Brackens	K2
17	St Andrew's Sq Nth	L12	39	Stockdam Road	C19	21	Summerhill Park	S12	38	The Brambles	B20
17	St Andrew's Sq West	L12	26	Stockman's Ave	H14	21	Summerhill Pde	S12	3	The Cairn	K2
3	St Anne's Cres	J2	26	Stockman's Court	H14	32	Summerhill Place	F17	20	The Cairns	R11
3	St Anne's Mews	J2		(Cuirt Mhic Giolla Stoic)		32	Summerhill Road	F17	5	The Cedars	N2
12	St Aubyn St	M9	26	Stockman's Cres	H14	19	Sunbury Avenue	Q12	28	The Cloisters	M13
11	St Colmban's Ct	K10	26	Stockman's Drive	H14	29	Sunderland Road	P14	43	The Close	E22
22	St Elizabeth's Ct	U11	26	Stockman's Gdns	H14	11	Sunningdale Dr	K8	23	The Close	V13
34	St Ellen's	J17	26	Stockman's Lane	H14	11	Sunningdale Gdns	K8	33	The Close	H16
11	St Gemma's Ct	K10	26	Stockman's Park	H14	11	Sunningdale Grove	J8	44	The Close	T6
17	St George's Gdns	L12	26	Stockmans Way	H14	11	Sunningdale Green	J8	33	The Crescent	H17
18	St George's Harbour	M12	2	Stoke Road	G3	11	Sunningdale Park	K8	44	The Crescent	T6
16	St Gerard's Manor	G12	21	Stoney Road	T11	11	Sunningdale Park Nth	K8	32	The Cutts	E18
27	St Ives Gardens	L14	10	Stoneycairn Ct	H8	11	Sunninghill Drive	K8	7	The Diamond	M4
17	St James's Court	M14	19	Stonyford Street	P11	11	Sunninghill Gdns	J8	19	The Drive	L15
16	St James's Drive	J12	21	Stormont Court	S12	11	Sunninghill Park	J8	20	The Earls Court	Q11
17	St James's Gdns	J12	21	Stormont Mews	S12	33	Sunnyhill Park	F17	44	The Esplanade	S6
16	St James's Parade	J12	21	Stormont Park	S11	33	Sunnymede Ave	F17	5	The Firs	N2
16	St James's Place	J12	12	Stormont Road	N9	33	Sunnymede Park	F17	36	The Gables	N17
17	St James's Cres	J13	19	Stormount Cres	N12	28	Sunnyside Cres	M14	3	The Glade	K1
16	St James's Park	S12	19	Stormount Lane	N12	28	Sunnyside Drive	M14	9	The Glen	L9
17	St James's Road	J13	19	Stormount St	N12	28	Sunnyside Park	M14	38	The Grange	B19
11	St James's Street	L10	29	Stracam Corner	P14	28	Sunnyside Street	M14	15	The Grange	S10
28	St John's Mews	M14	44	Strand Avenue	S6	19	Sunwich Street	N12	42	The Green	C21
11	St John's Close	M11	18	Strand Close	N11	27	Surrey Street	K13	40	The Green	F19
15	St John's Court	M15	18	Strand Mews	N11	11	Susan Street	N11	33	The Green	G16
15	St John's Park	M15		(Eachlann na Tra)		18	Sussex Place	M12	42	The Green	C21
28	St John's Place	M14	44	Strand Mews	S6	3	Swanston Ave	H3	44	The Green	S7
28	St John's Wharf	M11	19	Strand Studios	P11	3	Swanston Cres	H3	44	The Grove	S7

STREET INDEX

Page	Street	Grid Ref
20	The Hamlets	R11
33	The Hawthorns	G16
32	The Hill	F18
33	The Hill	H16
20	The Hollies	Q12
33	The Laurels	H16
33	The Manor	G16
36	The Mews	M17
19	The Mount	N12
7	The Oaks	M4
38	The Oaks	C19
38	The Paddock	B20
33	The Park	F16
23	The Park	V13
5	The Pines	N2
35	The Plateau	K16
	Piney Hills	
29	The Silvergrove	P14
44	The Spires	T7
14	The Stables	R10
29	The Straight	N14
29	The Village Green	P13
34	The Vines	H16
14	The Walled Gardens	R10
29	The Willows	P15
17	Theodore Street	K12
29	Thiepval Avenue	P14
42	Thiepval Road	D21
17	Third Street	K11
17	Thirlmere Gardens	K8
19	Thistle Court	N11
38	Thistlemount Park	B20
32	Thomas Street	L10
13	Thompson Wharf Rd	N9
7	Thorburn Park	L5
7	Thorburn Road	L5
11	Thorndale Ave	L10
19	Thorndyke Street	N12
39	Thornhill Avenue	C19
32	Thornhill Court	F17
39	Thornhill Crescent	C19
32	Thornhill Crescent	F17
21	Thornhill Crescent	S12
21	Thornhill Drive	S12
27	Thornhill Gardens	K14
39	Thornhill Gardens	C19
21	Thornhill Grove	S12
27	Thornhill Malone	K14
33	Thornhill Manor	F17
21	Thornhill Mews	S12
21	Thornhill Parade	S12
39	Thornhill Park	C19
21	Thornhill Park	S12
32	Thornhill Road	F17
42	Thornleigh Close	C21
42	Thornleigh Drive	C21
42	Thornleigh Park	C21
42	Thornleigh Place	C21
6	Throne Terrace	L5
17	Tierney Gardens	L2
25	Tildarg Avenue	F15
14	Tildarg Street	N13
14	Tillysburn Drive	R9
14	Tillysburn Grove	R10
14	Tillysburn Park	R9
41	Timbey Park	M14
41	Tirowen Crescent	B22
41	Tirowen Drive	B21
41	Tirowen Way	B21
29	Titania Street	N13
7	Tivoli Gardens	K8
3	Tobarcooran Avenue	K3
3	Tobergill Street	K10
11	Tokio Gardens	K8
25	*Tollnamona Court	G13
	(Altnamona Crescent)	
18	Tomb Street	M11
18	Tomb Street	M11
42	Tonagh Avenue	C21
42	Tonagh Drive	C21
42	Tonagh Mews	C21
42	Tonagh Park	C21
18	Toronto Street	N12
11	Torr Way	H15
11	Torrens Avenue	K9
11	Torrens Court	K9
11	Torrens Crescent	K9
11	Torrens Drive	K9
11	Torrens Gardens	K9
11	Torrens Parade	K9
11	Torrens Road	K9
23	Torrin Walk	V12
19	Tower Court	M11
29	Tower Street	N11
19	Tower Street	N11
18	Townhall Street	M11
17	Townsend Street	L11
19	*Townsley Street	P11
	(Manderson Street)	
18	Trafalgar Street	M10
42	Traherne Gardens	D23
12	Trainfield Street	L10
17	Tralee Street	J11
29	Trassey Close	N14
25	Trench Avenue	G15
2	Trench Lane	F3
25	Trench Park	G15
2	Trench Road	G2
25	Trenchard	F15
44	Trevor Street	S7
29	Trigo Parade	P13
19	Trillick Court	N12
19	Trillick Street	N12
42	Trinity Gate	D21
38	Trinity Square	B20
18	Trinity Street	L10
42	Trinity Terrace	D21
34	Trossachs Drive	H17
34	Trossachs Drive	H16
33	Trossachs Gdns	H17
33	Trossachs Park	H17
42	Trostan Place	C21
25	Trostan Way	H14
38	Troutbeck Avenue	B20
29	Tudor Avenue	P14
5	Tudor Avenue	N2
20	Tudor Dale	Q10
29	Tudor Drive	P14
39	Tudor Grange	C20
5	Tudor Grove	N2
44	Tudor Oaks	T6
29	Tudor Park	F2
11	Tudor Place	K9
25	Tullagh Park	G14
4	Tulleevin Drive	M3
4	Tulleevin Walk	M3
30	Tullyard Way	Q14
	(Heichbrae Airt)	
25	Tullymore Drive	G14
25	Tullymore Gdns	G14
25	Tullymore Gdns	G14
25	Tullymore Walk	G14
40	Tullynacross Road	F20
39	Tullyvar Park	C20
17	Turin Street	K12
10	Twaddell Avenue	J10
21	Tweskard Lodge	S10
21	Tweskard Park	S10
32	Twinbrook Road	E16
4	Twinburn Cres	M1
4	Twinburn Drive	M1
4	Twinburn Gardens	M1
4	Twinburn Hill	M1
4	Twinburn Park	M1
4	Twinburn Road	M1
4	Twinburn Way	M1
44	Twiselside	T6
5	Tynan Close	N1
5	Tynan Drive	N1
10	Tyndale Crescent	J8
10	Tyndale Drive	J8
10	Tyndale Gardens	J8
10	Tyndale Grove	J8
10	Tyndale Green	J8
39	Tynedale Crescent	C20
39	Tynedale Park	C20
17	Tyrone Street	L11
	(Sraid Thir Eoghain)	
33	**ULSTER AVENUE**	G17
18	Ulster Street	M11
19	Ulsterdale Street	P12
17	Ulsterville Ave	K13
17	Ulsterville Drive	K13
17	Ulsterville Gdns	K13
27	Ulsterville Place	K13
18	Union Street	L11
19	Uniondale Street	P12
28	University Ave	M13
17	University Road	L13
18	University Sq	L13
18	University Sq Mews	L13
18	University Street	L13
27	University Tce	L13
18	Upper Arthur St	L11
31	Upper Braniel Rd	S14
17	Upper Canning St	L10
8	Upper Castle Park	K7
8	Upper Cavehill Rd	K7
17	Upper Charleville St	K10
18	Upper Church Lane	M11
18	Upper Crescent	L13
24	Upper Dunmurry Lane	F16
33	Upper Dunmurry Lane	F16
19	Upper Frank St	N12
29	Upper Galwally	N15
17	Upper Glenfarne St	K10
33	Upper Green	G16
8	Upper Hightown Rd	J7
6	Upper Hollybrook Hts	
	(see insert)	
29	Upper Knockbreda Rd	P14
29	Upper Knockbreda Rd	N15
30	Upper Knockbreda Rd	Q14
26	Upper Lisburn Road	J15
34	Upper Malone Cl	J16
34	Upper Malone Cr	J16
34	Upper Malone Gdns	J16
34	Upper Malone Pk	J16
34	Upper Malone Rd	H17
37	Upper Malvern Crescent	P16
37	Upper Malvern Drive	P16
37	Upper Malvern Park	P16
37	Upper Malvern Road	P16
12	Upper Meadow St	L10
17	*Upper Meenan Street	K10
	(Sancroft Street)	
12	Upper Mervue St	L9
21	Upper Newtownards Rd	S12
22	Upper Newtownards Rd	U11
18	Upper Queen St	L11
17	Upper Riga Street	K11
24	Upper Springfield Rd	E13
27	Upper Suffolk Rd	E14
21	Upperlands Walk	T12
3	Uppertown Drive	J1
17	Upper Stanfield St	M12
17	Upper Townsend Terrace	L11
33	Upton Avenue	H16
25	Upton Cottages	H13
16	Upton Court	H13
33	Upton Park	H16
17	Utility Street	L12
17	*Utility Walk	L12
	(Utility Street)	
6	**VADDEGAN AVE**	K4
6	Vaddegan Drive	K4
6	Vaddegan Gardens	K4
6	Vaddegan Park	K4
6	Vaddegan Road	K4
11	Valleyside Close	J11
11	Vancouver Drive	L8
9	Vandyck Crescent	L6
9	Vandyck Drive	L6
9	Vandyck Gardens	L6
17	Vara Drive	J11
28	Vauxhall Park	L15
11	Velsheda Court	J9
11	Velsheda Park	J9
10	Velsheda Way	J9
39	Ventnor Park	D19
18	Ventry Lane	L12
18	Ventry Street	L12
16	Vere Foster Walk	H11
18	Verner Street	M12
18	Vernon Court	L12
18	Vernon Street	L12
9	Veryan Gardens	L6
19	Vicarage Street	N11
11	Vicinage Park	L10
11	Vicinage Place	L10
18	Victor Place	N12
14	Victoria Avenue	Q10
11	Victoria Court	Q10
43	Victoria Crescent	E21
19	Victoria Drive	Q10
33	Victoria Gardens	G17
11	Victoria Gardens	K8
12	Victoria Parade	L10
14	Victoria Road	N10
19	Victoria Road	Q10
44	Victoria Road	T6
11	Victoria Square	M11
18	Victoria Street	M11
43	Victory Street	E21
19	Vidor Court	Q10
19	Vidor Gardens	Q10
34	Viewfort Park	H17
36	Village Court	M16
3	Village Court	K2
17	Violet Street	K12
21	Vionville Close	T13
21	Vionville Court	T12
21	Vionville Green	T12
21	Vionville Heights	T13
21	Vionville Park	T12
21	Vionville Place	T12
21	Vionville Rise	T12
21	Vionville View	T12
21	Vionville Way	T13
18	Virginia Street	L12
18	Virginia Way	L12
11	Vistula Street	K10
9	Voltaire Gardens	L6
19	Vulcan Court	N11
	(Cuirt Bholcain)	
18	Vulcan Gardens	N11
	(Gairdini Bholcain)	
18	Vulcan Link	N11
	(Lub Bholcain)	
18	Vulcan Street	N11
	(Sraid Bholcain)	
5	**WALL STREET**	N3
17	Wall St	L11
	(Sraid an Bhalla)	
11	Wallasey Park	J8
19	Walker Court	N12
43	Wallace Avenue	E21
40	Wallace Mews	C21
28	Walmer Street	M14
18	Walnut Court	M12
18	Walnut Mews	M12
18	Walnut Street	M12
20	Wandsworth Ct	R11
20	Wandsworth Cres	R11
20	Wandsworth Dr	R11
20	Wandsworth Gdns	R11
20	Wandsworth Pde	R11
20	Wandsworth Pl	R11
20	Wandsworth Rd	R11
28	Wansbeck Street	L14
22	Wanstead Ave	U13
23	Wanstead Court	V13
23	Wanstead Drive	V13
22	Wanstead Gdns	U13
22	Wanstead Mews	V13
23	Wanstead Park	V13
23	Wanstead Road	V13
42	Ward Avenue	C22
42	Wardsborough Road	D21
18	Waring Street	M11
42	Warren Close	C22
42	Warren Gardens	C22
30	Warren Grove	R13
42	Warren Grove	C22
42	Warren Park	D22
42	Warren Park Avenue	D22
42	Warren Park Drive	C22
42	Warren Park Gardens	C22
17	Warrenmount	C22
17	Waterford Gdns	K11
17	Waterford Street	K11
17	Waterford Way	K11
9	Waterloo Gardens	L7
9	Waterloo Park	L7

STREET INDEX

Page		Grid Ref	Page		Grid Ref	Page		Grid Ref	Page		Grid Ref
9	Waterloo Pk Nth	L7	10	Westway Drive	H10	17	Wilton Gardens	K11	7	Woodland Terrace	N4
9	Waterloo Pk Sth	L7	10	Westway Gardens	H10	17	Wilton Street	K11	44	Woodlands	T6
16	Watermouth Cres	J11	10	Westway Gardens	H10	17	Winchester Court	K10	38	Woodlands Close	B20
42	Waterside	D22	10	Westway Grove	H10	37	Windermere Ave	P16	20	Woodlands Court	R11
17	Waterville Street	K11	10	Westway Park	H10	37	Windermere Close	P16	38	Woodlands Court	B20
12	Watkins Road	M10	10	Westway Parade	H10	37	Windermere Cres	P16	38	Woodlands Mews	B20
17	Watson Street	L12	10	Wheatfield Cres	H9	37	Windermere Drive	P16	19	Woodlee Street	P12
19	Watt Street	L12	10	Wheatfield Drive	J9	11	Windermere Gdns	K8	42	Woodside	D22
17	Wauchope Court	J12	10	Wheatfield Gdns	J9	37	Windermere Green	P16	32	Woodside Drive	E16
9	Waveney Avenue	L7	32	Whin Park	E17	37	Windermere Park	P16	32	Woodside Park	E16
9	Waveney Drive	L7	30	Whincroft Road	R13	38	Windermere Road	B20	32	Woodside View	E16
9	Waveney Grove	L7	30	Whincroft Way	R13	37	Windermere Road	P16	32	Woodside Walk	E16
9	Waveney Hts	M7	36	Whinney Heights	N16	37	Windermere Village	P16	18	Woodstock Link	N12
9	Waveney Park	L7	35	Whinnyhill Drive	L17	37	Windrush Avenue	P16	18	Woodstock Place	N12
42	Waverley Avenue	D22	32	White Glen	D16	37	Windrush Park	P16	18	Woodstock Road	N12
3	Waverley Avenue	K1	32	White Rise	D16	42	Windsor Avenue	C22	38	Woodvale	B19
42	Waverley Cres	D22	16	Whitecliff Cres	H12	44	Windsor Avenue	T7	17	Woodvale Ave	J11
3	Waverley Cres	K1	16	Whitecliff Drive	H12	27	Windsor Avenue	K13	10	Woodvale Drive	J10
3	Waverley Drive	K1	16	Whitecliff Parade	H12	27	Windsor Ave Nth	L13	10	Woodvale Gdns	J10
3	Waverley Gardens	K1	28	Whitehall Gardens	M14	27	Windsor Close	K14	17	Woodvale Pass	J11
3	Waverley Grove	K1	28	Whitehall Mews	M14	27	Windsor Court	K14	10	Woodvale Parade	J10
3	Waverley Park	K2	28	Whitehall Parade	M14	27	Windsor Drive	K13	11	Woodvale Road	J10
3	Waverley Road	K1	42	Whitehill Lodge	C21	27	Windsor Manor	K13	10	Woodvale Street	J10
19	Wayland Street	P12	7	Whitehouse Gdns	N5	27	Windsor Mews	K14	42	Woodview Cres	D22
30	Wayside Close	R13	7	Whitehouse Park	N5	27	Windsor Park	K14	42	Woodview Drive	D22
16	Weavershill Lane	H8	16	Whiterock Close	H12	27	Windsor Road	K13	31	Woodview Drive	S13
10	Weavershill Walk	H8		(Clos na Carraige Baine)		27	Windsor Street	L12	31	Woodview Place	S13
33	Wedderburn Ave	H16	16	Whiterock Cres	H12	18	Winecellar Entry	L11	31	Woodview Tce	S13
33	Wedderburn Gdns	H16	16	Whiterock Drive	H12	35	Winetavern St	L11	16	Workman Avenue	J11
9	Well Place	N1	16	Whiterock Gdns	H12	19	Wingrove Gdns	P12	13	Workman Road	P9
19	Welland Street	P11	16	Whiterock Grove	H12	20	Winston Gardens	R12	5	Wye Street	N11
27	Wellesley Ave	L13	16	Whiterock Parade	H12	19	Witham Street	P11	20	Wynard Park	R12
18	Wellington Court	L12	16	Whiterock Road	H12	10	Wolfend Drive	H8	29	Wynchurch Ave	N15
27	Wellington Park	L13	9	Whitewell Cres	L6	10	Wolfend Way	H8	29	Wynchurch Close	N15
27	Wellington Park Ave	L13	13	Whitewell Drive	L6	19	Wolff Close	N11	29	Wynchurch Gdns	N15
27	Wellington Park Mews	K13	6	Whitewell Mews	L4	13	Wolff Road	P9	29	Wynchurch Park	N14
27	Wellington Park Tce	L13	9	Whitewell Parade	M6	10	Wolfhill Avenue	G8	29	Wynchurch Road	N15
27	Wellington Park Tce	L13	7	Whitewell Road	L5	10	Wolfhill Ave Sth	G8	29	Wynchurch Tce	N15
18	Wellington Pl	L11	39	Whitla Crescent	D20	10	Wolfhill Drive	G8	29	Wynchurch Walk	N15
18	Wellington St	L12	39	Whitla Road	D20	10	Wolfhill Gardens	G8	42	Wyncroft Cres	C21
19	Wellwood Ave	P10	17	Whitla Street	M10	10	Wolfhill Grove	G8	42	Wyncroft Gdns	C21
19	Wellwood Close	P10	17	*Wigton Street	K11	18	Wolseley Street	L13	11	Wyndham Drive	K9
17	Wellwood Street	L12		(Dover Place)		44	Wood End	S7	11	Wyndham Street	K9
18	Welsh Street	M12	40	Wilden Street	E20	5	Wood Grange	P2	19	Wynfield Court	Q11
17	*Wesley Court	L12	27	Wildflower Way	J14	5	Wood Green	P2	43	Wynford Park	E22
	(Donegall Road)		20	*Wilgar Close	Q11	32	Wood Side	F18	19	Wynford Street	P12
17	*Wesley Street	L12		(Wilgar Street)		44	Woodbank Lane	T6	3	Wynnland Ave	J2
	(Donegall Road)		20	Wilgar Street	Q11	24	Woodbourne Court	F15	3	Wynnland Cres	J2
43	Wesley Street	E21	28	Willesden Park	L15	24	Woodbourne Crescent	F15	3	Wynnland Drive	J2
13	West Bank Close	P8	33	William Alexander Pk	G16	36	Woodbreda Ave	N16	3	Wynnland Gdns	J2
13	West Bank Drive	P7	18	William Street	L11	36	Woodbreda Cres	N16	3	Wynnland Park	J2
13	West Bank Road	P8	18	William St South	M11	36	Woodbreda Drive	N16	3	Wynnland Road	J2
13	West Bank Way	P7	33	Willisfield Avenue	H16	36	Woodbreda Gdns	N16	7	Wynthorp Grove	N4
42	West Court	C21	33	Willisfield Gdns	H16	36	Woodbreda Park	N16			
14	West Circular Crescent	H11	33	Willisfield Park	H16	11	Woodburn Drive	K8	11	YARROW COURT	K10
16	West Circular Road	H11	33	Willow Cottages	F18	30	Woodcot Ave	P12	11	Yarrow Street	K10
7	West Crescent	L4	33	Willow Court	F18	30	Woodcroft Hts	R14	33	Yew Street	J10
44	West Green	S7	33	Willow Gardens	G18	30	Woodcroft Rise	R14	33	Yew Tree Walk	F17
44	West Link	S7	7	Willow Park	M4	5	Woodfield	N1	12	York Crescent	M8
42	West Park	C21	17	Willow Street	L12	5	Woodfield Drive	N1	12	York Drive	M8
19	Westbourne St	N11	29	Willowbank Cres	P15	5	Woodfield Glen	N1	18	York Lane	L11
19	Westcott Street	P12	29	Willowbank Drive	N15	5	Woodfield Grange	N1	18	York Link	M10
16	Westhill Way	H12	11	Willowbank Gdns	L9	4	Woodford Ave	K1	12	York Park	M8
11	Westland Drive	K8	29	Willowbank Park	N15	4	Woodford Cres	K1	12	York Parade	M8
11	Westland Gardens	K9	19	Willowfield Ave	N12	4	Woodford Drive	K1	12	York Road	M9
11	Westland Road	K9	19	Willowfield Cres	N12	4	Woodford Gdns	L1	18	York Street	M10
11	Westland Way	K8	19	Willowfield Drive	N12	36	Woodford Green	N17	43	Young St	E21
17	Westlink	K12	19	Willowfield Gdns	N12	4	Woodford Grove	K1	5	Ypres Park	N3
17	Westlink	L11	19	Willowfield Pde	N12	4	Woodford Manor	L1	19	Yukon Street	P11
19	Westminster Ave	P11	19	Willowfield Street	N12	4	Woodford Parade	K1			
19	Westminster Ave Nth	P11	19	Willowfield Walk	N12	4	Woodford Park	K1			
18	Westminster St	M13	19	Willowholme Cres	N13	4	Woodford Park East	K1			
26	Weston Drive	J15	19	Willowholme Dr	N13	4	Woodford Road	L1			
16	Westrock Court	H12	19	Willowholme Pde	N13	38	Woodglen	B20			
16	Westrock Cres	H12	19	Willowholme St	N13	44	Woodgrange	T6			
16	Westrock Drive	H12	2	Willowtree Park	G2	40	Woodland Avenue	E19			
16	Westrock Gardens	H12	23	Willowvale	V12	11	Woodland Avenue	L9			
16	Westrock Green	H12	25	Willowvale Ave	G15	5	Woodland Close	N4			
16	Westrock Parade	H12	25	Willowvale Gdns	G15	5	Woodland Cres	N4			
16	Westrock Park	H12	25	Willowvale Mews	G15	7	Woodland Drive	N4			
16	Westrock Place	H12	32	Wilmar Road	E18	39	Woodland Drive	E19			
16	Westrock Square	J12	34	Wilmont Park	H17	39	Woodland Gardens	E19			
16	Westrock Way	J12	14	Wilshere Drive	R10	25	Woodland Grange	G15			
16	Westview Pass	H12	43	Wilson Street	E21	42	Woodland Park	D22			
10	Westway Cres	H10	17	Wilson Street	L11	40	Woodland Park	E19			
	(Wastairt Bowe)		17	Wilson's Court	L11	40	Woodland Park North	E19			
			17	Wilton Court Mws	K11	5	Woodland Place	N4			